The Modern Traveller to the Early Irish Church

The Modern Traveller
to the Early Irish Church

❖

Kathleen Hughes and Ann Hamlin

FOUR COURTS PRESS

Published by
FOUR COURTS PRESS
55 Prussia Street, Dublin 7, Ireland
and in North America by
FOUR COURTS PRESS
c/o ISBS, 5804 N.E. Hassalo Street, Portland, OR 97213.

The first edition of this book was published in 1977 by SPCK.
This new edition was published in 1997

A catalogue record for this title
is available from the British Library.

ISBN 1-85182-194-5

Printed in Great Britain
by Hartnolls Ltd, Bodmin, Cornwall.

Contents

ACKNOWLEDGEMENT

Thanks are due to Constable & Company Ltd for permission to quote four verses from 'The Monk and his Pet Cat' from *Selections from Ancient Irish Poetry*, translated by Kuno Meyer

List of illustrations

These figures are not measured drawings but are based on photographs by Seán Goddard and Ann Hamlin, except for those for which acknowledgement is made in the Introduction. Where like material is grouped on a page a uniform scale has been used.

Introduction to the 1997 edition

This book was published in January 1977 and was reprinted in New York in 1981 but has been out-of-print since 1988. Only a few months after the book's appearance Kathleen Hughes, the senior partner, died at the sadly early age of 50 (on 20 April 1977). She was the foremost student of early Irish church history of her generation and her work has profoundly influenced scholars who have followed her.

Why should a book published nearly 20 years ago be reprinted and offered once again to the public? I would maintain that the need which we set out to meet in the mid 1970s still exists and that the book will still have a role. We aimed to answer the questions which people visiting early Irish ecclesiastical sites would ask, writing for a wide general readership but basing the text on sound evidence and careful use of source material. Year by year there are more travellers to early Irish ecclesiastical sites, and more students begin the study of the history and archaeology of the early Irish church, so there may well be a continuing place for our small guide.

It is left to me, as the surviving author, to resolve how best to revise the book to take account of the gap of almost 20 years since its first publication. The study of the early Irish church has advanced dramatically, with the publication of editions of important sources and a steady flow of other publications, including historical studies, excavation reports, survey volumes and a major *corpus* of crosses.

Rather than attempt to revise the main text, I have decided to indicate in this introduction one of the main ways in which the study has advanced, and also to point the reader towards some of the publications which have appeared since 1977.

There is a strong emphasis in the text on the monastic church. Since Kathleen Hughes's death, and building in part on the found-

ix

ation she laid, scholars have developed a more complex 'model' which includes not only large and small monasteries, but also episcopal centres, where bishops were based, old missionary churches, churches belonging to families or population groups, small 'proto-parish' churches (centres for pastoral work and burial), and isolated hermitages, as well as sites at which several different elements coexisted. Monasteries, therefore, formed only part of a very much more varied and complex picture. In practice what this means for the visitor, I suggest, is that the sites mentioned in the text and listed as 'recommended' probably span the whole range I have indicated - from complex ecclesiastical settlements in which monastic and secular elements coexisted, through large and small monasteries, to family, group or 'parish' churches and isolated retreats. If you substitute the adjective 'ecclesiastical' for 'monastic', you leave open the wide range of possible kinds of establishments which current scholarship now indicates.

In a small book which covers 700 years or more, there is inevitably a great deal of generalisation. We were aware of this problem, and it was pointed out in several reviews. The 'broad brush' approach was deliberate, but the suggestions for further reading allow exploration in more detail, including chronological refinement where this is possible.

The guidance on access in the 'List of recommended sites', especially boat access to islands, needs to be checked locally as conditions change, and notes on the state of sites ('neglected', for example) may be out-of-date. Places to visit should now include several recently-opened visitor centres with displays interpreting the early Irish church, including Clonmacnois, Glendalough, Nendrum and Devenish.

September 1996   ANN HAMLIN

Introduction

Early Irish clerics liked to think about heaven, to imagine what it would be like. But Christians had to build the church on earth, and that building was conditioned by their geography, economy and institutions. The church in Ireland does not look quite the same as the church elsewhere, because circumstances in Ireland were different. Almost all western Europe was shaped to some extent by the legacy of Rome; but the imperial armies never reached Ireland, and the church here was little affected by Roman bureaucracy or law, even by Roman building-styles or art.

Some of the remains of the Irish church can very easily be seen, whereas early English churches have often been overrun by industrialization. It requires a great effort of imagination to reconstruct Bede's physical world out of the bleak buildings on the outskirts of modern Jarrow (Co. Durham), or to envisage the seventh-century community at Escomb to the south-west in its present decayed nineteenth-century mining village, even though the churches are there. But rural Ireland is thinly populated, and the monastic settlements which the modern traveller will probably find most pleasure in visiting, standing on their islands or headlands, or rising from the shores of empty bays or on the banks of rivers, can with a little information be repeopled. A hundred yards outside the monastic enclosure the physical experience is the same for us as it was for them: 'A clear-voiced cuckoo sings to me', the sound of the 'white-waved sea' is unchanged. Sometimes this is enough, but some people also seek an intellectual experience, to understand the physical world and the motives and conditions of the people who once lived there. This small book is a brief attempt at explanation.

We should like to acknowledge help with Chapter 3 from Dr A. T. Lucas and Dr Fergus Kelly, and with Chapter 6 from

Father Brendan Bradshaw, S.M., and to thank our friends who have read and criticized the text. We are grateful to Liam de Paor for permission to use his section of Cell A, Skellig Michael (Fig. 14), and the Dundalgan Press for allowing us to use H. G. Leask's sections of stone-roofed churches (Fig. 9). We also thank the following institutions for permission to reproduce their treasures: The National Museum of Ireland (the Lough Lene Bell, Fig. 12, and *Breac Maodhóg*, Fig. 4), the Board of Trinity College Dublin (the church in the temptation scene from the Book of Kells, Fig. 7), the Ulster Museum (the Bann crozier, Fig. 12), the Stiftsbibliothek St Gall (the St Matthew figure from Codex 1395, Fig. 1), the President and Fellows of Corpus Christi College, Oxford (the Corpus Missal and satchel, Fig. 1). The other figures are based on photographs by Seán Goddard and Ann Hamlin. None are measured drawings.

The first three chapters are by Kathleen Hughes, the last three by Ann Hamlin, though each of us has criticized and contributed to the other's section. Ann Hamlin has been mainly responsible for the list of recommended sites and has planned the illustrations, which have been executed by Seán Goddard.

29 September 1975   KATHLEEN HUGHES
                                       ANN HAMLIN

1

Function

Why did people go into monasteries in early Ireland? What were monasteries for? There was a religious reason, and there were a number of complementary sociological reasons. The religious one comes first in time, indeed, it determines the foundation of monasteries; but by the eighth century, when Christianity had been fully integrated with native institutions, the part which the monastery played in society as landlord, purveyor of social services and patron of the arts was prominent. Then and later it was the ascetics who sustained the spiritual tradition laid down by the founders in the sixth and early seventh centuries.

There is no complete philosophy of the monastic life in early Irish records, but if the sermons attributed to Columbanus are really by him they provide the fullest early statement. Columbanus, a monk of Bangor, went as an exile for Christ to the Continent and founded houses at Annegray, Luxeuil and Bobbio, where he died in 615. The monastic life as he sees it is for contemplating and practising the presence of God. For him Jesus is the joy of man's desiring, and to long for God is greater bliss than any worldly pleasure, any earthly fulfilment: 'Taste and see,' he says, 'how lovely, how pleasant is the Lord.' It is the language of the mystic, yet this experience is within the scope of all monks, for the monk is to unite himself to God, a theme on which Columbanus writes often. 'May no one and nothing separate us from the love of Christ . . . that we may abide in him here' and for ever; 'Live in Christ, that Christ may live in you'; 'Thou gavest thyself for us. Wherefore we beseech thee that we may know the thing we love, since we pray for nothing other than thyself to be given to us.' The monk must be completely committed, in such a state that 'we may contemplate thee alone by day and night and always hold thee in our thoughts'. Such a condition is one of infinite joy, for 'love is no trouble', 'love is its own health'.

1

But loving God requires the cultivation of certain qualities, and this needs 'application and toil'. This is what the ascetic life is for. The true disciple must be in the same state as Christ, stripping himself of worldy goods, 'satisfied with the small possessions of utter need'. Columbanus is deeply aware of human sin, and this is where the modern sociologist or psychologist finds him very unsympathetic. 'It requires great violence to seek by toil and to maintain by exertion what a corrupted nature has not kept'. For Columbanus the flesh is 'unclean by nature', the body is a prison, and the monk must fight in Christ's host against the vices which constantly assail him. The idea of physical self-discipline to reach some goal is practised in our own society by athletes, some of whom, such as boxers or climbers, are prepared to undergo physical damage; the early Irish ascetic welcomed physical hardship, but for a different end. Columbanus' Penitential (the schedule of penances allotted for various sins) is the most brutal of all the Irish penitentials. In the Rule which he wrote for his monks he lays down three stages in the monastic life: first, the practice of asceticism, by which the monk strips himself of self, which leads him to the second stage, 'the purging of vices' so that he finally reaches 'the most perfect and perpetual love of God.'

Nowhere else is the statement so coherent as in Columbanus' writings, but there are many texts which illustrate and elaborate this philosophy, monastic Rules, poetry, saints' Lives, voyage tales and vision literature. The ascetic life does not always appear such a harsh and grim affair as it does in Columbanus' work: elsewhere it is 'the urging and kindling of men . . . to serve the Lord', in which the saint is 'compelled by Christ'. Moreover, severe asceticism was maintained by comparatively few. Irish monasticism accepted that men had different gifts and different capacities, and God did not call them all to the same degree of discipline.

The vision of God, to be submerged in the enormous bliss of his presence, was the goal, and the texts speak constantly of it. It will be the saints' delight in the life to come. One tenth-century writer envisages the saints in these terms: 'They have need of nothing but to be listening to the music to which they listen, and

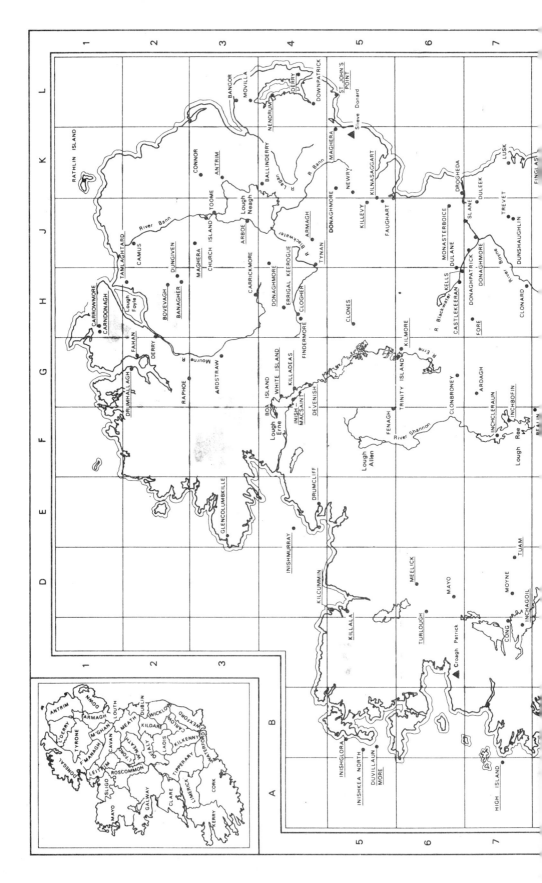

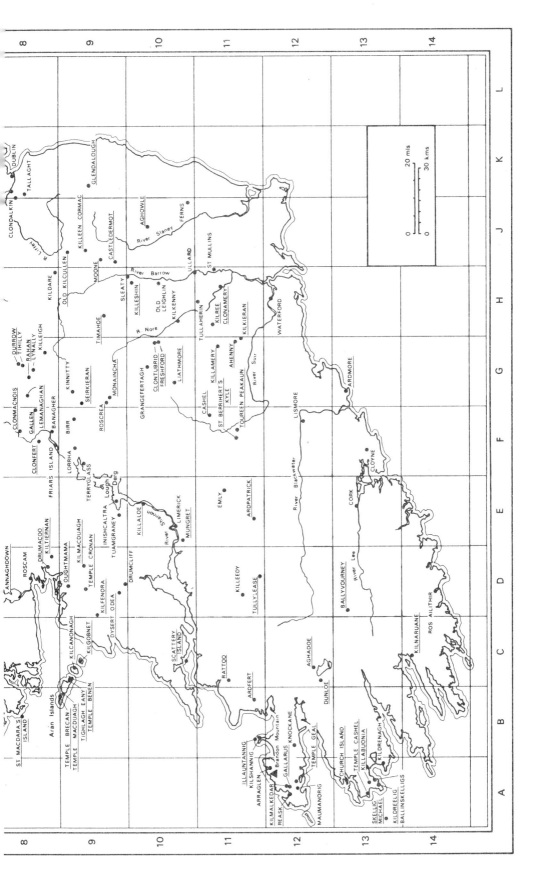

to look on the light which they see and to be filled with the fragrance which is in the land'. In this vision the Lord is seated on a blazing throne, before him three birds: 'and their minds are set on their Creator through the ages, that is their art'. The Lord himself is indescribable: 'None can tell his ardour and his energy, his blazing and his brilliance, his splendour and his bliss, his constancy and steadfastness'. The monk's hope is to be one of that 'household of heaven'.

But the presence of God is not only something for the future; it is something which may be enjoyed now, if only transitorily. 'God is near to all who call upon him', says one woman saint, and when a rather tiresome young man asks her to state precisely in what position a man ought to pray, lying or sitting or standing, she answers briefly: 'One must pray in every position'. Another abbess says: 'You are the habitation of God, body and spirit', and advises a girl to persist in prayer and meditation. Brigit says: 'From the hour I set my mind on God I never took it away from him'. The saints are the people who have this intimacy with God. Brendan, for instance, is likened to John, 'the Lord's bosom-fosterling'; Íte is the woman saint to whom Jesus comes in the form of a babe, no mere commoner (the Irish saints are intensely aristocratic) but the King of Heaven, for, as she says, 'He is in his place on high, though as little Jesus he is on my breast.' One poet prays: 'Be thou my vision, beloved Lord . . . Be thou alone my heart's special love; let there be none other save the high-king of Heaven.'

These men also see God in the natural world, another form of contemplation. One of them looks out from his island over the sea, listening to the waves breaking on the rocks, to the gulls' cry, watching the smooth strand of clear headlands, the splendid bird-flocks, the mighty whales, blessing the Lord 'who has power over all'. He sits here 'a while meditating upon the Kingdom of Heaven'. Another exclaims: 'Let us adore the Lord, maker of wondrous works, great heaven bright with its angels, the white-waved sea on earth.' Yet another sits with his open book under a hedge of trees, with a blackbird to sing to him: 'The Lord is indeed good to me.'

3

Birds and beasts may be the messengers of God. One day when Brendan was alone in the church a great longing for God seized him. Then the archangel Michael came to him in the form of a bright bird and perched on the window (there would have been no glass) and sang him sweet music, and Brendan was listening to it until the same hour next day, when Michael bade him farewell. So his longing was satisfied by the music of heaven. One of the most entrancing scenes in the story of the Voyage of Brendan is that of the great fish (porpoises perhaps?) who surround Brendan's boat while he is singing mass, 'crowds of swimming forms', then, when mass is over, leap away. A boar was St Ciarán's first disciple, joined by a fox, a badger, a wolf, and a hind. A doe came to be milked by Ruadán, and stags drew various saints' plough-teams. A sea-otter brought fish and firewood to Paul the Hermit, alone on his island. The fox is the bad dog of saints' Lives, overcome by greed: Ciarán of Seir's fox steals his slippers, Ciarán of Clonmacnois's fox, overcome by his 'natural treachery', starts to chew his psalter, liking the taste of the vellum (the leather on which it was written). These are literary conventions, but they show a kindness between man and the natural world, as a common part of God's creation.

It is often angels who form the link between men and God. Angels are over and around a holy place, constantly passing up and down between it and God, and men who have spoken with them come back with their faces radiant. Columcille says he loves Derry 'because it is full of white angels from one end to the other'. Irish angels are mirthful, in fact, they are often noisy, singing loudly, playing instruments. They come and run races for the monks of Colmán when they have been disappointed in being unable to attend the fair of Telltown. The household of heaven, in some writings at least, is a merry community in God's 'royal hall'.

This, then, is the religious ideal which drew men and women into monasteries—the desire for God and the joy which his presence offers. At least it is part, and the most attractive part, of the picture. But one can hardly escape the fact that some writers saw the ascetic life as an expiation, by which men must atone for their sins in order to reach heaven. This idea is not, of course, peculiar to Ireland, but Irish law, like other barbarian legal systems, may help to explain why it gained support, for the secular law saw misdeeds as injuries which had to be compensated and paid for. So sin has to be paid for by mortification, a man must 'make satisfaction', sin gives rise to an 'obligation', penance is the way by which a man's guilt 'may be remitted to him'. People were constantly aware of the uncertainties of life, and some were oppressed by ideas of sin and judgement. It may not be chance that monasticism seems to have gained many adherents after the terrible plague which swept over Ireland in the mid-sixth century, which took a heavy death toll and was remembered for long afterwards.

Of course the religious life was not only a personal and private communion between man and God. It was structured by acts of community worship. The daily services of the church were collectively called the *opus dei*, or the 'hours', for they were held at certain fixed times during the day. The number of 'hours' (the offices) varies in Irish documents from six to eight. In winter the night is long and the day short, so the night 'hours' are lengthy and the day 'hours' brief; in summer the reverse is the case. It will be least confusing if we imagine the monastic day at the summer or winter equinox (20 March or 23 September), when the day and night are of equal length. The monks went to bed when the sun went down, slept and then rose for nocturns, the night office, round about the middle of the night. At dawn they attended lauds. The three daytime hours are terce, sext (midday) and none, that is the third, sixth and ninth hours, and on the sundials to be seen on various sites these hours are marked (Fig. 21). Vespers was said in the evening. This gives six 'hours'. Occasionally tracts refer to compline and prime, which seem to be the prayers said on going to bed and rising. One manuscript explains why these 'hours' are kept: terce because Christ was given up then to Pontius Pilate, sext because then he was put on the cross, none because at that hour he died. Mass was celebrated on Sundays and feastdays, probably after terce. The monks were summoned to the church by the bell: one ninth-

5

century poem speaks of the 'sweet-sounding bell ringing on a windy night' to call the monk to his tryst.

Piety has completely changed its image since the early middle ages. The Irish saints were not meek and mild: indeed some are depicted as violent, vengeful, mighty cursers. But this is incidental. The central feature of all saints is that they are men of power, who have access to the power of God. This is why they can cure the sick, raise the dead, bring a boat safely through a storm, calm a ferocious beast, beat off a raiding army, and do all the other things that ordinary mortals cannot do. By the seventh century a cleric commanded a high honour price (which determined his legal rights and privileges as well as his social position). He was usually from one of the aristocratic strata of society, often related to the local nobility. Some had inherited the prophetic and visionary powers of the druids, and they shared the prestige of men of learning, so that everything combined to build up a popular impression of status and power. The men living in these monastic settlements were not the misfits, the naturally humble and retiring; they were the social élite.

Not all the monks in an Irish monastery led an ascetic and celibate life. As far as we can see the land for a monastic foundation was often provided by the agreement of the whole kin group. In early times a man could not at his own will grant family land away outside the kin. What may have happened, at any rate in some cases, is that the family as a unit made over its land to found a monastery. Then some of the family led a religious life of prayer, asceticism, saying the office (the church services). They formed the inner circle of administrators and ascetics, and included a bishop or priest (sometimes several), the abbot, the steward, the head of the school. Some monasteries seem to have consisted only of these people, and the monks acted as farm labourers. But we know that some houses from the beginning had lay monks called *manaig*, who lived with their wives and farmed the land: they or their ancestors were probably living on the land when it was first made over to the monastery. Such laymen had to make one major change, for early Irish society had been polygamous, and the married layman who formed part of

6

the monastic society had only one wife. Thus some 'monks' were actually born into the system. Their living was on the monastic land, and it would have been very difficult for them to leave. They attended church services on Sundays and on major feasts, and their eldest sons were educated with a clerical education in the monastic school. They did not make any decision to enter monasticism, and they followed a very modified form of the monastic life.

Perhaps of all these people the only ones who can be said to have deliberately chosen a particular style of life were the ascetics. To some extent all the rest were ushered into their careers by inheritance and education. A monastery must be seen as an estate, directed to a religious purpose, but on which only some people, at times comparatively few, led an ascetic life. Even the abbot might be married, and if so his descendants often held the abbacy after him. Thus the question 'Why did people go into monasteries?' needs to be re-phrased. We should rather ask 'What were monasteries for?'

The historical development of monasticism provides part of the answer. There were men and women in Ireland leading an ascetic life in the fifth century, perhaps living in communities, but the administration of the church was in the hands of bishops, as it was elsewhere in Europe, who ruled dioceses coterminous with the petty kingdoms into which Ireland was divided. Ireland received its first bishop in 431. Then, about the middle of the sixth century, families seem to have founded a number of monasteries which fairly quickly grew into the kinds of establishment which I have described, and which superseded the diocesan bishoprics. There were bishops living in these monasteries to ordain and consecrate and perform other sacramental functions, but by about 700, probably considerably before, the government of the Irish church was in the hands of abbots. So when we think of the Irish church we must think of a monastic church which performed spiritual duties for the laity—baptism, the saying of mass, preaching and burial. What you see throughout the Irish countryside today is the remains of that church.

We might digress here to ask what about the women? Until

very recently society has offered few opportunities to women, and the religious life has always had a special appeal for them. Some monastic writers seem to have been rather nervous of women. The Life of Senán tells how one woman wanted to come and take up the religious life with him on his island (Scattery Island near the entrance to the Shannon harbour). Senán was very reluctant to admit her, and she gives the most spirited defence of women in religion that I know of in early Irish ecclesiastical literature:

> Christ is no worse than you. Christ came to save women no less than men. He suffered for the sake of women no less than for men. Women have given service and ministry to Christ and his apostles. Women enter the heavenly kingdom no less than men.

After this Senán had to let her enter.

There were many women in early Ireland following a monastic life, for a calendar written about 800 names scores of them who are to be remembered. Yet we only hear of four women's foundations which survived as major monasteries over a long period, Kildare, Killeedy, Killevy, and Clonbroney. This is probably partly because, in the early period, a woman could only have a life interest in land which she inherited, and at her death it passed back to her kin. She could gain land in perpetuity, but not family land; she could only hand on outside her kin that land which she received as a gift or gained for services rendered. In early times men could not grant away family land either, without the consent of their kin, but they had better opportunities for gaining wealth by their own efforts than women had. The Irish law of inheritance probably explains the discrepancies between the large number of holy women and the tiny number of well-known women's houses. We should imagine a lot of small establishments for women at any one time, but they must have broken up on the death of the woman who had provided the endowment.

Kildare is the most famous of all the women's houses. It was founded before monasticism became popular, and it always had an important bishop. When we see it in the seventh century, it supported a community of nuns and also a group of clerics who lived separately. The nuns in other women's houses do not ap-

8

pear to have been strictly enclosed: Samthann, founder of Clonbroney, talks to monks and scholars, while Íte of Killeedy seems to have had a monastery similar to the population-centres I have described, with married laymen living on her monastic property, one a craftsman married to Íte's sister. The abbess is prepared to support a nun with an illegitimate child, and she meets outsiders: there is an amusing story of how she puts down an arrogant young cleric who thinks his masters are wasting their time visiting that old maid. Such a house seems to have functioned like other Irish monasteries, with a mixed population of ascetics, administrators, and lay families.

Íte is the saint who is renowned in legend and poetry as the foster-mother of Christ, and fosterage is one of the social functions which a monastery performed. The upper classes of society sent their children away to be fostered: it was probably the more desirable in a society where a man might have children by different women, and where a child's mother might not be the father's 'chief wife'. The secular law laid down what children were to be taught, and how much fosterage-fee was to be paid. Children fostered in a monastery formed part of the abbot's household and received an ecclesiastical education in the monastic school. Those we hear of often became clerics. Fosterage was one of the ways in which Irish monasticism maintained close links with secular society, for the relationship between foster-parent and child was usually one of affection. In the saints' Lives we see princes putting out their sons to be fostered in monasteries, and going to visit them to see that all was well, and we find phrases used such as 'he loved him greatly' to describe the abbot's attitude to his fosterling.

Formal education was provided by the monastic school. Boys were taught in a Latin, ecclesiastical tradition. They learned the Latin language, and study of the notes and marks in manuscripts shows how Irishmen tried to help themselves with the more difficult aspects of the Latin texts they were using. Here we can get very close to the Irish student or master as he tries to guide himself through the various elements in a long Latin sentence, putting in Irish translations of Latin words. We have one

9

seventh-century book of model verse-compositions, which gives incidental information about the monastic economy (see p. 52), and there are treatises on Latin grammar as early as the seventh century. Serious study made some Irishmen fluent Latinists who enjoyed playing with words.

But the first textbook which all boys used was the Psalms. Irish clerics constantly recited the Psalter: they loved its poetry, and probably accepted its violence and vengeance as a norm. One of the earliest of all our Irish manuscripts (early seventh century) is a Latin Psalter ascribed to Columcille of Iona, called the *Cathach* or 'Battler' because it used to be carried into battle. It is now in the Royal Irish Academy at Dublin and its eleventh-century shrine is in the National Museum.

Good monastic libraries contained copies of the Scriptures, of some of the church Fathers, of some classical works, and some history and letters. We have to reconstruct their libraries from the works which authors quote, and we cannot always be sure that they had a complete text. But we can see them at work copying texts. Columcille insists that when the copying is finished a work has to be checked against the original to make sure of its accuracy, a very necessary precaution. A miniature in an Irish manuscript now at St Gall in Switzerland shows a seated scribe with an ink-horn fixed to his chair, a pen in his right hand and a pen-knife in his left, while another figure (the evangelist?) reads to him from a book, presumably supplying the inspiration by which he is to write (Fig. 1).

The monastic scribe might also be an illuminator, for important books, especially the Gospels which lay on the altar, might be illuminated. Sometimes several illuminators were at work on the same manuscript. The Book of Durrow (seventh century) and the Book of Kells (a little later), two of the most splendid of such illuminated books, are both on view at Trinity College, Dublin. There is dispute as to where these books were written: wherever it was, it must have been in a centre where Irish, Northumbrian and, in the case of Kells, Pictish influences were all apparent. There are also smaller illuminated books, like the Book of Mulling or the Book of Dimma (both in Trinity College, Dublin) which are known as 'pocket gospels'. They, or less splendid ones somewhat like them, may have been kept in leather book satchels hanging in the library, or in some privileged monk's cell. There is such a book satchel in Corpus Christi College, Oxford (Fig. 1). An important monastery probably had at least one splendid illuminated book like the one which Giraldus the Welshman in the twelfth century tells us he saw at Kildare, 'with almost as many drawings as pages, and all of them in marvellous colours'. He

Fig. 1   Seated scribe, satchel and book

says: 'If you take the trouble to look very closely, and penetrate with your eyes to the secrets of the artistry', you will notice delicate and subtle intricacies, still fresh in their colouring. The inspiration and expertise of the artists is still evident today.

The scribes and learned men were not merely copying and illuminating; they were composing. Up to about 800 it was mainly grammar books and commentaries on the scriptures, service books, litanies, calendars (lists of saints arranged under the days of the year), church legislation, annals, and Lives of some

11

Irish saints. Such works were mainly in Latin and must have been for a restricted audience, just those with a clerical education. After 800 the language becomes increasingly Irish; the audience which could enjoy such literature must have widened, and the subject-matter broadens in character. In the pre-Christian period Ireland had had a learned class of 'poets', who kept the traditions and genealogies and stories of the aristocracy, and the monastic church had never entirely cut herself off from these men, for poets visited the monasteries on their travels and sang their songs to the monks (as we can see in the seventh-century Life of Columcille). As the church became more and more adapted to Irish conventions some of its literature showed increasingly the influence of native traditions. The voyage tales, for instance, in which a saint sets off with his crew to seek the Land of Promise on an island in the ocean, borrow from Irish legend, and some of the saints' Lives have qualities in common with the hero-tales. The heroic literature, much of which is pagan in morality, must have been preserved in the monasteries and was certainly known to the monks: one twelfth-century satire tells how the hermit comes out of his cell with the heroic tales of fightings and wooings stuffed in his boots! The monks probably viewed this heroic literature as the past history of their people. They also turned the pre-Christian gods into earlier inhabitants of Ireland, whose invasions they synchronized with Old Testament events to produce a great scheme of history. Thus Ireland has kept an unusually rich early literature and lore, and the imaginative ideas of church writers were stimulated by the secular tradition.

So we can imagine the monk writing in Irish and Latin, enjoying his tales of fantasy and marvels, composing lyric poetry, systematizing past tradition, hunting up Greek and Hebrew words and providing philological explanations, and settling down to the study of the Scriptures. One, in the ninth century, likens his intellectual activities to the life of his cat (I quote part of the poem in Kuno Meyer's translation):

> I and my white Pangur
> Have each his special art:

His mind is set on hunting mice,
Mine is upon my special craft.

I love to rest—better than any fame!—
With close study at my little book:
White Pangur does not envy me:
He loves his childish play.

He rejoices with quick leaps
When in his sharp claw sticks a mouse:
I too rejoice when I have grasped
A problem difficult and dearly loved.

Though we are thus at all times,
Neither hinders the other.
Each of us pleased with his own art
Amuses himself alone.

The monasteries, then, in addition to their primary religious purpose, were places for fosterage and centres of education and learning. They also fulfilled another important social function, since they provided patronage for the arts. Ireland had skilled metalworkers, who provided brooches, belt-fastenings and equipment for the aristocracy, and once the church became established and wealthy, it began to need fine equipment (see p. 49). If art is to flourish and develop, there must be people who can pay for its production. Beautiful and elaborate objects like the Ardagh Chalice or the Moylough belt-shrine (both on exhibition in the National Museum, Dublin) must have taken months to produce, and years of skilled practice lie behind them. The craftsmen who made them were either permanent or temporary residents on the monastic estate.

The church not only displayed fine objects, but a monastery must also have been a kind of bank. Ireland was a society without a coinage, but obligations were partly met by 'gifts', and contracts were initiated by the exchange of pledges, which took the form of some precious or semi-precious object. A monastery must have had its own little hoard of such pieces, and it seems quite likely also that it kept them in safe custody for other people, for the monastery provided sanctuary, and was protected by law from violence. This does not mean that people never invaded its sanctuary. We read of fairly numerous occasions in the annals when they did, sometimes in search of a particular man who was being hunted down; but until the Viking raids began in the ninth century a general sack of a church was not usual, its possessions were not desecrated, and after the invasion life went on as before. War was endemic in Irish society, and until the ninth century church sanctuary seems to have been generally observed.

Moreover, there is some evidence which suggests that, when times were troubled, ordinary lay-folk might bring their own valuables inside the monastic enclosure, thereby hoping to keep them safe. 'Valuables' would not necessarily be metalwork: indeed, the man who could afford fine brooches would probably have a well-enclosed farmstead of his own, and men to fight with him to protect it. But stocks of corn were sometimes brought into the monastic enclosure to keep them safe, and of course a big monastery had its own corn and seed stocks, which had to be enough to feed a sizeable population. So the monastery, as well as being a bank for a collection of metalwork, was also a granary, safer than most others until the Vikings arrived in the ninth century. From the tenth century onwards the Irish themselves frequently joined in attacks on churches, and the old sacred inviolability had gone.

Right through the early middle ages the Irish monasteries dispensed hospitality. It was, of course, a Christian duty, the more necessary when there were no hotels. As we shall see, monasteries often lay on or near main routes, so they were obvious stopping-places. But hospitality was also an obligation of secular law. There was a special class of person in Irish law whose duty was to dispense universal hospitality, and every freeman had a legal obligation to supply hospitality (though not to those of higher class than himself), the food provided varying with the rank of the guest. Refusal of hospitality was a grave offence, involving heavy fines. Monastic hospitality was therefore both a Christian obligation and a secular requirement. Poets and clerics could move about the country freely, not held by the boundaries of their own petty kingdoms; local kings sometimes had their own

14

residences in monasteries as they did at Durrow and Armagh. For these and other travellers the monasteries provided temporary living. When a twelfth-century satirist wanted to jeer at the monks of Cork he abused their hospitality; he said he had found there a wind-swept, draughty house, dirty bedding full of lice and fleas, and the last night's bathwater still in the tub, his commons a small cup of whey and a miserable oatcake. Brigit's prayer was to be able to provide generous hospitality:

> I should like a great lake of ale for the King of kings.
> I should like the household of heaven to be there
> drinking it for eternity . . .
> I should like cheerfulness to be in their drinking,
> I should like Jesus here also.

The monastery had a worldly reputation, like any other noble, and its hospitality must be up to the approved standard.

There is one more social function a monastery fulfilled. It was a kind of open prison, for a large monastery had a group of penitents attached to it. Some of these had committed major injuries against society, such as murder. It would be safer for a murderer to leave the world and seek the protection of a monastery where he would have to follow a penitential regime but where his life would be secure, than to live in the world where he might have to pay the ultimate price to vengeance. This is the nearest thing to a prison which early Irish society had.

Monasteries were, then, primarily places for the pursuit of a religious life. This is why they were founded, and there were always some people who chose a life of asceticism and religion, sometimes more, sometimes fewer. But some monasteries were family foundations, and they provided a livelihood for members of the kin. They were also places of fosterage, education and learning, providing patronage for the arts and safe-keeping for treasures. They played the part of hotels, and to some extent even of prisons. They were an integral part of early Irish society.

Once the church ceased to be a tiny group of believers and became an institution, it was fairly quickly adapted to native legal and social requirements. Certain aspects of Christian theology must have been easy for the Irish to grasp, while others were obviously very difficult, for social conventions would facilitate or frustrate understanding, as they do in any society to which a new religious philosophy is introduced.

The miracle-stories of the New Testament, which present so great a difficulty for a modern rationalist audience, were meat and drink to the early Irish, as to most other barbarian peoples. They delighted in marvels and were ready to believe them. Druids had had powers of prophecy and second sight; why not saints? They were ready to believe in another world, and the people from that world sometimes came back to meet with men. So, though the Irish pagan other-world is not a spiritual but a very material one, with warriors and women and entertainment, the Irish did not find the conception of a life outside this present one at all impossible.

There were other concepts which today are almost mere words, but which then had immediate relevance. The Irish were passionately concerned with their family and ancestry: who a man's father was had an importance almost inconceivable in a modern egalitarian society where a man is valued for what he is and does himself, regardless of his relatives and forebears. So when an Irishman was told he was a son of God, an heir of God, one of the family of God, it must have been the most proud and triumphant news. Christ had shared his glory with them, as a scholar noted, in Irish, in his copy of the Pauline epistles.

The lordship of Christ also had meaning in terms of contemporary institutions, for free society was made up of lords and clients. The free clients were the lord's companions, attended him in his hall, fought for him; the lord provided protection and entertainment, gave the feasts. So when an Irishman took God as his lord all these ideas of the relations between lord and client lay behind his statement. One group of reformed religious in the late ninth century actually called themselve *céli dé*, 'clients of God', the men who had taken God as lord.

Other Christian concepts were, however, obviously extremely difficult to grasp. Secular society was aristocratic, and status was one of its basic concepts. Men of honour had to insist on their

16

rights, and to keep their place in society with proper pride. The monastic Rules constantly enjoin humility, submission; the monk must 'keep silence when he has suffered wrong'; the contentious man is to 'subject himself to the decision of another'; there is to be no boasting or vainglory. Yet often the saints in the later Lives are the opposite of all this. They fiercely contest their rights (as an honourable hero would have done), they worst their opponents, they boast their prowess (again according to the traditions of heroic convention). We see the church teaching the precepts of the Sermon on the Mount to the devout, yet when the saint has to be presented to a public audience he is often clothed in the garb of the hero. So holy men, in maintaining their claims against each other, might start with a boasting match; sometimes they fought like heroes, and the saint might show the conventional phenomenon of the warrior, the hero's light on his brow. Christian teaching and accepted convention were in some cases opposed, and the men who administered the monasteries or wrote the saints' Lives were deeply steeped in conventions, and sometimes presented their patron in popular guise.

Monasteries not infrequently went to war, sometimes in self-defence, but sometimes under conditions where at least one side must have been the aggressor. But fighting was part of the life of an Irish aristocrat, and a man showed his honour by his readiness and skill as a fighter. So a precept such as 'Blessed are the peacemakers' might run counter to the ethic of earlier Irish society, where peacemaking in certain conditions was absolutely proper, but where revenge for wrong suffered was equally necessary if order was to be maintained. In establishing claims to sanctuary and in providing a possible life for non-fighters the church in fact improved the condition of society.

Catholic theology was taken over completely by the Irish: there is very little trace of heresy. Christianity as it was taught to monks was based firmly on the New Testament and the Church Fathers, and the monks spent time studying the Scriptures and commenting on them. But monasteries were not made up only of scholars and ascetics. They were a part of society, close to their own kin, to the nobility, aware of competition and pressure. So

17

when administrators wanted to maintain and advance the financial rights of their own house, they depicted their patron saint as a man of power in a conventional pattern, cursing as well as blessing. This does not invalidate the real evidence we have for the monastery as a centre of personal religion, asceticism and contemplation, nor the evidence for the church as a beneficent social force, working alongside secular institutions, providing education and learning, patronage for art, hospitality and fosterage.

2

Sites

Many Irish monastic sites could be visited for the delight of the experience. They are often superbly situated, in the bend of a river, on green southward-facing slopes, or looking out over bays and headlands, so that brightness seems to fall on them. But the traveller may want to know why they were built precisely there, and whether the whole pattern of monastic sites shows any significant features.

Perhaps originally the choice of a site was a fairly haphazard affair, but the ones which lasted—and that is usually the ones we know about—survived because they fulfilled certain requirements. Those requirements varied, for some houses were ascetic and contemplative communities, while others played an important part in everyday society, so we should not expect to find them all in the same kind of place.

The isolated houses, remote from men, are often the ones which have survived best. The most dramatic of all, which the traveller will want to visit, is on the Great Skellig, Skellig Michael, 'the steep rock of Michael'. This is a triangle of rock, about 2,000 ft from end to end, rising abruptly out of the sea about eight miles from the coast of the Waterville Peninsula in Co. Kerry. The peak is 715 ft above sea level, and the monastery is on a shelf just beneath the north-eastern height. The lighthouse staff on the rock now land by helicopter, but tourists travel out by boat from a number of places along the coast when the weather is favourable.

This seems a most unlikely place for a monastery, for the western seas are rough, and approach by curragh (the boats made of skin stretched over a wicker frame which the monks used) can never have been easy. But there was a settlement here, not just a hermitage; there are six cells, two chapels, and a little graveyard high up on the shoulder of the island, with a tiny garden. It is a long and in places a rather dizzy climb up the stone stairs from the harbour to the monastery. Early medieval men obviously felt that Michael was at home in steep little islands and on hilltops— there are famous mounts off the southern coast of Cornwall near Penzance, or the north coast of Brittany and a chapel dedicated to him on Glastonbury Tor—but nowhere else is the site so spectacular as on the Irish Skellig Michael. The traveller is reminded of the poem on St Brigit, who 'sat the perch of a bird on a cliff'. That is what these monks must have done.

Life in a community like Skellig Michael must have been contemplative, not active. Once the building was finished there was comparatively little the monks could do—a little gardening, hunting for birds' eggs, fishing—but most of the time must have been given to prayer. In rough or misty weather they were even out of sight of the land, lost in cloud and storm. The graveyard has never been excavated, so we do not know how many men lie buried here, though there are a number of slabs; nor do we know for how long the community lasted, though the cells (Fig. 14) are not all constructed in the same style, and may not all belong to the same date. Was this a summer retreat, or an all-the-year-round monastery? There was certainly someone here in 824 when Etgal of Skellig Michael was carried off by the Vikings, and died soon after of hunger and thirst.

There are other monasteries in remote places, although no other site is as dramatic as the Skellig. One, comparatively well preserved, is on Inishmurray, about four miles off the coast of Sligo. Nearly all Irish monasteries are within an enclosing wall either of earth (a rath) or stone (a cashel), but on Inishmurray the cashel is of quite unusual size, comparable to the walls of secular forts like Staigue or Ailech, so that it is possible that the monastery took over some lord's cashel. It is a sizeable enclosure with internal walls dividing the main area from three smaller and separate areas, which were possibly used for specific purposes, and about fifty cross-slabs lie inside and outside the enclosure. This monastery is mentioned in the annals (though they deal mainly with other areas), so it was clearly known throughout Ireland. All the same, it could only be reached with considerable

20

effort, and it seems likely that the community here lived very much separate from the world, and was little concerned in public affairs until the Viking raiders forced it into a front-line position, very accessible to seafarers.

Small islands provide very suitable sites for ascetic communities who wish to maintain their isolation. This is presumably why monks founded a house on the tiny Church Island in Valencia Harbour (Waterville peninsula), where the monastic wall skirts the perimeter of the island whose habitable surface is only about four-tenths of an acre. On a mild and calm day this monastery could easily be in touch with the nearby mainland, but there are strong tidal currents, and in rough weather when a heavy swell comes in from the Atlantic access must have been difficult or impossible.

There are also sites on the mainland in remote positions. Kildreelig, for instance, is high on a headland between Ballinskelligs and St Finan's Bay (Waterville peninsula). It is not easy to find, but it is worth looking for, as it has marvellous views, looking east over Ballinskelligs Bay to Waterville and Lough Currane, south across the sea to the islands of Scariff and Deenish, while away to the west is Skellig Michael. There must once have been a monastery here, with a thick circular enclosure wall and an outer terrace; two upright stone slabs guard the outer entrance, and a church, cross-slabs, a souterrain and collapsed huts are within the inner enclosure. It stands near the edge of the cliff, and can never have been easily accessible either by land or sea.

The mountain-top hermitage or church is unusual, but some are striking enough to attract attention. Slieve Donard, the highest peak in the Mourne Mountains, gets its name from a·saint who built his hermitage on its top: it was probably in a prehistoric megalithic cairn. On the summit of Mount Brandon on the Dingle peninsula is the ruined hermitage of St Brendan, with oratory, cells and a well inside an enclosure, and the top of Croagh Patrick (Co. Mayo) is now a pilgrimage site. Such sites must always have been deliberately difficult of access.

Monasteries or hermitages like this were built by ascetics who wanted a place remote from the world, near cliff and cloud, within sight of rocks, waves and islands, open to wind and sea. There were other ascetic sites in the forests, built of wood so that they have not survived. We know of them from the poetry, like the one more delightful than any mansion, thatched by 'my dear heart, God of Heaven', a place in which spears are not feared. Another hermit writes under his wall of forest, and the cuckoo, in grey hood, calls from bush-citadels; for another the blackbird sings in the thicket.

Although these ascetic sites are the ones which catch the imagination, whether by sight or words, nevertheless they are not really typical of the Irish church—or, at least, they are only typical of one aspect of it. There are many settlements which look remote now, but were not so then. Nearly all the major sites which grew into important monasteries with long histories are in easily accessible places, on major routes. Some are coastal sites on sea routes. Nendrum on Mahee Island in Strangford Lough (a sea lough) is on a small island (now joined to the mainland by a road) and could be approached by land or sea. There was clearly once a major settlement here, with three concentric enclosure walls. The excavated finds prove that there was a monastery here by the eighth century, and the chancel, added to the church in the twelfth century, shows that the site was in use then. (The imaginative reconstruction, Fig. 5, is based on the surviving and excavated remains of this monastery.) To the north, near the southern coast of Belfast Lough, a little upslope from the water is Bangor, one of the greatest of Irish monasteries in the seventh century, where now only later buildings survive. From here the monks could sail up the north-eastern coast of Ireland, then make the crossing of eighteen miles or so to the Irish-occupied land of Kintyre in Scotland, then through the islands to Iona or further north to Applecross on the mainland, both of which had important monastic houses. Or they could sail from Columba's monastery at Derry, down Lough Foyle and along the north coast, putting in at Rathlin Island before making the crossing to Kintyre and so to Iona.

On the south coast of Ireland there are comparable sites, where the sea gave easy access, not only to other places along the Irish

22

coast, but to Britain or the Continent. One of the fairest of all
these is Ardmore, where the monastery is at the head of a deep
bay, protected from rough seas and yet accessible to continental
travellers. The existing remains standing on a hill include a small
oratory ('Declán's cell'), one of the finest round towers in Ireland,
and a Romanesque church. Away on the headland, almost over-
hanging the sea, is the later pilgrims' church, probably built on
the site of Declán's hermitage. His Life relates: 'He was there in
his beloved cell which he had built himself, which is between the
hill and the sea in a narrow, secret place above the edge of the sea;
through which a clear little stream flows from the hillside into the
sea, and trees beautifully surround it.' This description could fit
the location of the pilgrims' church. The whole site well illustrates how a major monastery grew up in an accessible but
defensible situation, usually not right on the coast but near it, and
how a hermitage for ascetics might well be maintained in connection with it. It must have been monasteries like this which
received pilgrims from Gaul in the early middle ages. Further
south-west along the coast Ros Ailithir (Promontory of the
Pilgrim), in Ross Carbery Bay, was a well-known school.

Some of the most obvious natural routes lie along major rivers,
and monasteries are frequently found here. Inishcaltra on Lough
Derg must be reached by boat, but it was in fact on one of the
main highways of Ireland, up the Shannon from Limerick,
through Lough Derg and beyond, through Lough Ree up to
Lough Allen. Devenish is at the southern end of Lower Lough
Erne, and was easily accessible from the fifty-two miles of navig-
able waterway which form the Erne system. The low-lying lake
shores would have been damp and heavily wooded, so that water
transport must often have been easier than land travel. Devenish
had a long history: it was founded in the sixth century, rich
enough in the eleventh century to own a splendid reliquary,
Soiscél Mo-Laisse (the Gospel-Shrine of Mo-Laisse now in
Dublin in the National Museum), and still used as a burial-place
as late as the eighteenth century. The Lough Erne shrine,
dredged from the lake, presumably belonged to one of the local
monasteries. On the same lake there are a number of early sites,

such as Killadeas or White Island, both of which have unusual early figure carvings, or Inishmacsaint. The water here acted not as a barrier but as a main road to the monasteries.

The Barrow forms another major waterway in the south-east, flowing through a broad and beautiful vale between mountains, and here are a number of important monasteries. St Mullins, where kings of South Leinster sought burial, stands on a promontory, a naturally defensible site above the river. Old Leighlin, a hilltop site two miles west of the river, played a major part in ecclesiastical controversies of the seventh century, though the remains here are of much later date. Killeshin, where there is a splendid Romanesque west doorway, was an influential school, while Sleaty was another literary centre. A comparable important river site in the central south is Lismore, at the junction formed by the east-west route of the River Blackwater and the north-south route through the Knockmealdown Mountains to Cashel, the Munster capital. Cork lies further west at the mouth of the Lee and is a site which combines accessibility via the river to the interior with the advantages of a fine natural harbour.

The crossing-points of rivers were focuses for monasteries. Killaloe on the Shannon just below Lough Derg is an obvious example. Banagher (the shaft of whose high cross is in the National Museum, Dublin) is another house at a crossing-point on the Shannon, and there are early sites near the Bann fords at Toome, still an important bridging-point, and at Camus where the Bann approaches the sea. To this day some churches, like Kilkenny cathedral, stand above modern bridges where there must have been a ford or ferry at an early date.

Some of the natural routes follow glacial ridges, like the gravel ridge (esker) which divides the northern and southern halves of Ireland, and which is followed by a major prehistoric road. This road started in the east (near Dublin) and ran almost due west through Durrow to Clonmacnois. In the boggy land of central Ireland a well-drained glacial ridge provided the best trackway.

Some monasteries which at a superficial glance may look isolated were in fact at important road hubs. Glendalough, locked in by mountains, is just off a junction of important routes. The grand east-west route comes in by the Wicklow Gap, another north–south road approaches over the mountains by Lough Tay and Lough Dan (this is the most beautiful road from Dublin), or there is another road by the Vartry river, whilst from the south one arrives by way of the Vale of Clara. Once the modern traveller studies the map or, even better, takes the routes, he can well appreciate how a large monastery grew up here, important enough for kings to choose for their burying. There is a whole complex of sites on the upper and lower lake and further down the valley, covering a very large area and extending over a long period.

Some areas must have been a criss-cross of routes. There is a fertile area about 30 by 25 miles square to the east of the Shannon, shaped roughly like a parallelogram, bounded on the north and south by two ancient roads, on the south-east by highland and on the west by the Shannon (Fig. 2). This area is thick with major monasteries. Just north-east of Lough Derg are Lorrha and Terryglass. The Little Brosna river, one of the Shannon's tributaries, joins the Shannon a few miles north of Lough Derg, flowing from the south past Roscrea and Birr, whilst Seirkieran and Kinnitty are beneath the western side of Slieve Bloom, with Killeigh and Lynally to the north. Further north still are Tihilly, Rahan and Gallen, while Durrow and Clonmacnois lie on the glacial ridge-road. This whole area is well watered and fertile, and though most of the building must have been in wood, so that comparatively few early structures survive, some of the sites have some interesting features.

Roscrea and Monaincha, where the remains are Romanesque, are a good example of the way in which an ascetic community, as we know Monaincha once was, might be built within a couple of miles of a major monastery, Roscrea. The major house would then help to support the ascetics. The site of Monaincha was protected from the world by a lake called Loch Cré, and even today the church stands on a little island rising green from the middle of the bog. Seir and Rahan are interesting because they both show traces of the monastic enclosure, with banks and ditches particularly clear at Seir. Both these sites show how big an area might be covered by a major monastery, a very different affair from a tiny ascetic community like Kildreelig. Gallen and Durrow should be visited for their slabs and crosses, while

Fig. 2   Midland monasteries and early roads near the river Shannon

Clonmacnois (Fig. 22) is one of the most interesting monastic sites in Ireland.

The central-eastern plain is a comparable area to this territory east of the Shannon. Here there are also many houses, though only a few like Kells and Monasterboice have outstanding remains. This central-eastern area is also well watered, well

26

drained and fertile, and contains the natural meeting-points for routes—to Waterford Harbour in the South, to the south-west via Kildare, Roscrea and Killaloe to Limerick, west from Dublin to Durrow and Clonmacnois and beyond, with another western road from Drogheda through Kells and Fore to Rathcroghan, a prehistoric site associated with the Kings of Connacht. A road ran north from Drogheda to the Antrim coast, passing near Faughart and Kilnasaggart, then east of Lough Neagh, branching west at Antrim for Derry. The central-eastern plain was an obvious landing-place for travellers from Britain, as Dublin still is.

In this area the Boyne and the Blackwater form a major east–west route, coming out to the sea at Drogheda. Clonard is on one of the tributaries of the Boyne. The Blackwater is another tributary of the Boyne, flowing from the higher land to the north-west, past Castlekeeran with its three plain crosses, north of the hill-top site of Kells, one of the most important of all Irish monasteries, south-eastwards past Donaghpatrick (a *domhnach* church, see p. 29) which stands on a ridge, and joining the Boyne at Navan. Further east Slane, associated with St Patrick, occupies a commanding hilltop above the Boyne.

Rivers, passes and ridges were roadways, but monasteries were sometimes built on hilltop sites apart from the surrounding country yet in close relation to it, sites which in damp land supply dry 'islands' and sometimes have the attributes of a fort. Armagh, in a heavily glaciated area where there are well-drained hillocks in low-lying marshy surroundings, is an obvious example, and Cashel, rising abruptly from a plain, is now the most spectacular of all. Cashel is a focus of routes, to Roscrea and northwards, north-eastwards to Dublin, west to Limerick and south to Lismore and the coast. Cashel was a royal capital before it was an ecclesiastical site, and Armagh had pre-Christian associations, as its name indicates (see p. 30).

It is of course no accident that a medieval castle can sometimes be seen near an early monastery, for castle-builders wanted fertile, accessible yet defensible positions. The castle-mound at Clonard, like the church, is close to a main east–west road, and the mound near the church at Faughart overlooks the pass through the mountains known as the Gap of the North. At Clonmancnois a little down-stream is the ruin of a medieval castle, at Lynally a mound stands beside the church with a sixteenth-century castle visible a short distance away, and other examples might be named.

Monasteries which hoped to influence their society could not afford to indulge in hermit sites, but had to be in frequented places. St Cronán, in his Life, is said to have moved his monastery after people failed to find him: 'I will not be in a desert place where guests and poor people cannot easily find me, but I will stay here in a public place.' So he moved to Roscrea, and his monastery is now bisected by the road from Dublin to Limerick. The monastery's sociological functions could only be accomplished by a house built in an accessible position.

Clonmacnois (Fig. 22) is a very good example of a well-sited monastery, and this is why it grew to a position of such power and prestige. It is beside the junction of two major routes, the north–south route up the Shannon, and the glacial ridge route which ran across the centre of Ireland (Fig. 2). It covers a fair-sized area, bounded on one side by the river; it shows us a major monastery with an associated house nearby, this time a house for nuns, across a causeway (mentioned in the records) and down a lane, now the ruin of an attractive Romanesque building; it was an important burial-place, and has a fine collection of early grave slabs, well displayed; it was a patron of the arts, with two very fine high crosses and a third decorated cross shaft; it has a round tower, and nine churches of various dates. We must imagine the enclosure and the space immediately outside it as containing a lot of small houses, for we learn from the annals that in 1179 a hundred and five houses were burned here. This entry is just one of the many proofs that Clonmacnois, like Glendalough, Kells and other major sites, was a sizeable metropolis.

There are churches in areas which seem to belie the conditions of accessibility and fertility which I have claimed were necessary for the development of a major house. At first sight it looks as if the monasteries in the spectacular limestone country of Ireland, the Burren in the northern part of County Clare and the Aran

Islands, are in a desolate landscape, for this is a countryside of grey rock, where the light glitters on a sunny day, or where you may be lost in silent cloud. But there are greener hollows here, like the valleys where Temple Cronán and Oughtmama stand; excavation has shown that cattle-ranching communities lived in the many forts, and the number of enclosures, though they were probably not all in use at once, suggests a population with the necessary pasture for cattle.

The names of Irish monasteries often describe their sites: *inis* 'island', *cluain* 'meadow', *magh* 'plain', *ard* 'height'. *Cill* 'church' is very common, often followed by the saint's name, though there are other words for church, including *teach* 'house', *teampall* from Latin *templum*, *lann* like the Welsh *llan*, *díseart* 'retreat'. One of the most interesting is *domnach* from the Latin *dominicum*, for this belongs to a very early stratum of loan words, and the *domhnach* churches are thus some of the very earliest centres of Christianity in Ireland.

It has recently been argued by Dr Pádraig Ó Riain that monasteries were deliberately sited on the boundaries of kingdoms. The beautiful eighth-century crosses of Ahenny, Kilkieran and Killamery lie now on or near the boundary between Kilkenny and Tipperary, which must once have been the border between the kingdoms of Osraige and Éoganacht Caisil. Such examples could be multiplied. In putting monasteries in boundary zones the early Christians were following a tradition which saw those areas as suitable places for royal forts and public events such as fairs and assemblies. We also read in one early law text that the house of a man of learning was 'at the meeting of three streets'. But I think it is probable that forts and fairs and schools and monasteries were sited in boundary zones partly or even mainly because the routes ran there, and they needed to be in accessible places. It may also be that, just as Norman kings set up castles on their borders, so early Irish kings, much weaker, were glad to have monasteries there to provide areas of immunity.

There also seems to be some evidence that pagan religious activities had taken place in boundary areas. The god Lugh in one of the legends about places (*dindschenchus*) is supposed to have died at Uisnech, the place where five territories met; his divine slayers were themselves killed at Tailltiu near the Blackwater, which seems to have been the boundary line between the territories of the Fir Chúl Breg and Luigne. Pre-Christian inauguration rites seem often to have been held at meeting-places in boundary zones. One tract gives an account of a ritual curse uttered by the poets who repair 'at sun-rise to a height at the meeting point of seven territories', led by the *ollam* facing toward the territory of the king they wish to satirize, 'their backs to the thorn bush on the top of the height, and the wind from the north, and a casting (?stone) and a thorn from the bush in the hand of each man'. So there were already supernatural associations in the boundary zones before the monasteries were founded.

This brings us to another question: were monasteries often founded in places which had pagan religious associations? Two sites which have been interpreted as pagan sanctuaries have recently been excavated in Ireland. One, at Emain Macha (or Navan), is two miles from Amagh, dedicated to St Patrick, and Armagh itself takes its name, *Ard Macha* (the Height of Macha), from a pagan goddess: in the cathedral here are pagan carved stones. The other is at Knockaulin, five miles from Kildare, dedicated to St Brigit. We do not know who was worshipped at Knockaulin: was it the Irish goddess Bríg, 'the exalted one'? We know of a number of monasteries in Ireland where never-dying fires are specially mentioned. One of these was at Kildare, where Giraldus the Welshman in the twelfth century says that though the fire has never been extinguished for seven hundred years its ashes have never increased. (But the Archbishop of Dublin had it extinguished in 1220.) There were also said to be perpetual fires at Seirkieran, Kilmainham and Inishmurray. Fire seems to have played an important part in pagan ritual, and it must have been the texture of life for any community which lived solely on its own resources. Christianity did not eliminate the supernatural from Irish life; it merely traced it to a different source, so early Christians may well have been willing to take over sites already sacred in popular regard. It is exactly what Pope Gregory the Great tells the missionaries to the English to do. He says (as reported by Bede):

> I have decided after long deliberation . . . that the idol temples
> (of the English) should by no means be destroyed, but only the
> idols in them. Take holy water and sprinkle it in these shrines,
> build altars and place relics in them. For if the shrines are well
> built it is important that they should be changed from the
> worship of devils to the service of the true God.

Gregory recognized that people would go on coming to their
familiar places, so that it was necessary for the church to adopt
and adapt pagan sites to Christian uses. Theodore, the seventh-
century archbishop of Canterbury, passed legislation saying that
the bodies of pagans buried in Christian cemeteries were to be
exhumed, a ruling which suggests that Gregory's advice had been
adopted in England.

Some monasteries also seem to be connected with sacred trees.
St Finnian's monastery at Movilla (*Magh Bile*, plain of the tree)
or Brigit's at Kildare (*Cell-dara*, church of the oak wood) take their
names from trees. Patrick built a church near the sacred tree of
Tortan (*Bile Tortan*), which other sources tell us had been
planted from supernatural berries, and at Newry in Co. Down in
1162 there was a yew tree which Patrick himself was said to have
planted. Lorrha and Inishcaltra were said to have had miraculous
trees: the one at Lorrha produced a sap which tasted of wine and
satisfied whoever consumed it. The annals for 995 refer to the
sacred grove (*fid-nemed*) at Armagh, and the sixteenth-century
Life of Columcille implies that the oak-grove from which Derry
takes its name (*Daire*) was a sacred grove, whose trees must not
be cut: the sound of an axe in Derry was more frightening than
death, as one quatrain says.

The sacred tree was not confined to church precincts. Dr A. T.
Lucas has collected a large number of references which show
such trees in secular contexts, in the tales and in the annals. A
major fort sometimes had such a tree, and occasionally even took
its name from it, like Rathvilly (*Rath Bhile*), early centre of the
Uí Chenselaig. The inauguration rites of Irish kings were at
centres often connected with such trees, and in the annals round

about 980 (the event is differently dated in different versions) and at 1099 and 1111 we find references to the cutting down or uprooting by enemies of trees which are significant to a population-group. There can be no doubt from the wealth of evidence adduced that pagan sites had been marked by particular trees, and that Christian sites either took over the older sacred tree or that their own trees became sacred in popular regard.

A few of the early Christian sites are in close proximity to royal forts. Emain Macha was not only the sanctuary but the royal capital of the Kings of Ulaid, and Armagh, built so near, presumably had some connection with them; Derry is close to Ailech, capital of the Cenél Eógain Kings, Clogher to Rathmore, Dunshaughlin to Lagore. One Christian poet, writing about 800, comments on the way in which the old pagan sites have given way to monastic cities:

> The proud settlement of Aillin has died with its boasting hosts;
> Great is victorious Brigit, and lovely her thronged sanctuary.

But although we can point to a few monasteries in Ireland which must almost certainly have been founded under royal patronage, most of them seem to have been independent foundations on family land. Kings were weak at the time when monasteries were first being set up, so it is not surprising that most monastic sites have little relation to royal forts.

'Paganism has been destroyed' exults the ninth-century Irish poet, 'though it was splendid and far-flung.' But, as Charles Plummer pointed out in 1910, there are many features in the saints' Lives which may be regarded as pagan survivals, and in recent years anthropological studies have brought a better understanding of the transition from paganism to Christianity. Christianity introduced a new doctrine, a living way, so it had to be part of society, and its own members were of that society. People have never been wholly rationalistic, and it would be natural for them to transfer the sanctity of the old religion where possible to the new, as Pope Gregory recognized well enough. There is in fact less evidence in Ireland than one might expect for the adop-

32

tion of pagan sites by the church, but the saints abundantly provided their own aura of the supernatural.

By 800 the 'little places settled by two and threes' had become cities. One of the factors which determined whether a monastery would fade out or would grow in influence was its possession of the tomb of a powerful saint. The saint's body hallowed the ground, so that other people were eager to be buried alongside him, bringing burial-fees and wealth to the monastery. Burial-places in Ireland have always given entry to the other world: a twelfth-century writer described how the previous inhabitants of Ireland (who are in fact its euphemerized deities) retreated into the old burial-mounds when the Gael arrived. There they still dwell, as the local place-name legends told in the countryside abundantly testify.

It was therefore easy for an early medieval Irishman to see the monastic cemetery as the gateway to another life. Angels dwelt over it; ladders ascended from it to provide the way to that heavenly company. So the graveyard plays a central part in the life of the monastery, and also in that of the society, for not only did it act as a burial-place, but also oaths were taken there. Sometimes we can recognize the saint's tomb, as at Killabuonia on the Waterville peninsula (Fig. 3), where a triangular-shaped tomb formed of slabs stands near an engraved pillar outside the collapsed oratory (Fig. 6). This monastery is not mentioned in the records, for the annals have little to say about this part of Ireland and there is no Life of the saint, but it was clearly important. There are three terraces of walling, and the tomb has a central place within the inner enclosure. The slab at one end of the tomb is perforated by a round hole, presumably to allow the pilgrim to put in his hand and touch the relics. The tomb is now a net to catch the winds, and we do not know what saintly bones once slept there, but the saint's cult is still alive, for offerings may be seen in the well. This monastery, built on a southward-facing slope with a view of St Finan's Bay away to the west, within sight of the Skellig Rock, must once have been the major religious house of the area. The land about it is good pasture for cows, or suitable for haymaking.

33

Irish monastic sites show the variety and individuality of the Christian life. The houses which played the most important part in social life are nearly all in accessible places, on or near major land routes, in bays and harbours, in lakes which acted as waterways. Some, and they have tended to form the popular image, are genuinely remote: there may once have been more little places of the hermit type, but these rarely grew into monastic cities, surviving for many hundreds of years. Certain conditions were needful for growth. The founding saint had to be recognized as a man

Killabuonia

Banagher

Fig. 3   Special graves

of power, so that other people, in life and death, sought to be near his tomb. A great monastery had a sizeable population and needed enough fertile land to maintain it. The monastery had to be in a place to which people came, for hospitality and education, or where it might be convenient for a king to have a house. To such a house foreign pilgrims would come with their books and treasures, and it would become a library and a centre of literary production. Once a monastery began to grow in power it attracted further donations, or a popular school drew more scholars. The surviving texts allow us to see a church such as Armagh drawing up documents in the late seventh century in an attempt to establish her position as the major church in Ireland.

Irish monasticism always had its ascetics following the contemplative life. Popular literature, such as the saints' Lives, tends to present all monks as ascetics, but earlier and less biased evidence such as canon law and the secular law tracts shows clearly that they were not. The monastery was an institution in society, and its site expresses its function.

3

Economy

How did an Irish monastery maintain life? There is evidence to answer this question, though it is very scattered and fragmentary— usually incidental evidence in secular laws, monastic rules, saints' Lives, secular and ecclesiastical tales, and in a school-book used to teach advanced students a difficult and ornate form of Latin called *Hisperica Famina*. (On this text see the note at the end of the chapter.) A monastery was a subsistence-economy farm which had to produce almost all the things it needed, so we had better begin by seeing what the inhabitants ate (on which the documents are fairly specific) and what they wore; then we can consider what work had to be done, how the labour was recruited and organized and how the income was obtained.

Corn was a staple food for the laity as well as the clergy throughout the year. According to one of the Irish law tracts, the secular aristocracy (we have very little information about the poor) ate a considerable amount of meat during the winter months, mostly salt pork. Lent, at the end of winter, was a fairly lean time for everyone. Then from Easter on they ate 'summer food' which is glossed as cheese and butter, with green stuff from the garden as soon as it was available, honey and fruit. This suggests that milch-cows were the most valuable stock, which we know to be true from other sources. Pork is the prestige food in the sagas, usually the main dish, but beef is often mentioned and archaeology shows by the weight of beef-bones excavated that beef was eaten, so presumably young bullocks not needed for breeding purposes, once they were fully grown, would be killed off for meat. The lactation period in a cow now lasts up to ten months, but it is difficult to be sure how long it would have lasted then; probably not far short of this, for Irish pasture is good right up until the end of the year, and the animals were regularly milked. Only January and February were times of very thin pasture, when the cows grew lean.

Under modern conditions a sow farrows twice a year, but in early Ireland the sows would farrow probably once only, in the spring, and the pigs would find woodland pasture easily enough until January, feeding on the 'mast' which is frequently mentioned in the annals. From autumn onwards the pigs not needed for breeding purposes were killed, and the carcases dried and salted down for use as food. Sheep were kept for their wool, but they were also milked. From about March until December there was a fairly plentiful supply of milk, butter and cheese, with some meat, while from January until Lent salt meat was the main protein.

The monastic rules which we have relate mostly to the ascetics, and they ate less meat than the secular aristocracy. But one version of a tract says that even an ascetic community like the *céli dé* of Tallaght ate venison and wild boar and the monks were ordered not to hoard bacon and butter but to give them to the needy poor. Dairy produce was very important to the monastery, especially milk and butter, and cattle disease, which is sometimes mentioned in the annals, must have been a major disaster. The main monastic food supply was corn, made up into loaves or used in a kind of gruel made of meal and water and butter, so a good corn supply was essential. The seventh-century Life of Columcille tells how, when the saint felt death approaching in May, he went to bless the barn on Iona and was relieved and happy to see that there was enough grain to last out the monks until harvest. It seems likely that the growth of monasticism may have encouraged arable farming in Ireland, bringing more land under the plough.

The period after Easter must have brought improvement and variety in the diet as the garden produce came on, for it is called the season of 'the growth of the crops'. The Tallaght monks called it The Feast of the Ploughmen, when there was festivity and merry-making. We know of some of the plants cultivated in the garden: a vegetable like onions, one which may be carrot or parsnip, another which may be celery, some member of the cabbage family, peas and beans. As summer advanced wild berries, blackberries and strawberries ('good to taste in their plenty' as one hermit's poem says), nuts and cultivated apples, the main fruit of early Ireland, and possibly damsons were all available. Monasteries kept bees and hens; hens appear as decoration in the Book of Kells, eggs are described as 'the gems of a household', and excavation at Iona has uncovered the remains of domestic fowl, both hens and geese, as well as sea-birds.

One twelfth-century text from a monastic milieu, the Vision of Mac Conglinne, contains an enormous amount of information about food. It is by a man who had received a clerical education, and satirizes the abbot and monks of Cork for their sumptuous living. So, though the wandering scholar's meal is two small loaves and a slice of streaky bacon, the abbot is a gourmet, interested in a great range of foods made out of milk-products, cream, curds, buttermilk, many kinds of cheese, in different cuts of meat and different kinds of offal, in various vegetables and fruit, in cow's milk, ewe's milk, mead, ale, bragget (a kind of beer) and wine (which was presumably imported). When the scholar recites the abbot's ancestry, he insults him by reciting it according to the pedigree of food, since it is not his illustrious ancestors whom the abbot respects and reveres but a vast variety of foodstuffs. This text tells of a dish fit for a king, of meat dressed with honey and salt, with a honey sauce. The early Irish seem to have liked fatty foods served with plenty of gravy. Clerics who fed on such a diet must, like the aristocracy, have been large, solid, hearty folk, whereas the ascetics would be immediately recognizable by their much lighter weight.

A monastery near river or sea had fish in its diet, and it is clear that these were often caught systematically. At Iona there are piles of limpet, winkle, whelk and oyster shells; the cod and hake consumed here were up to twenty-five pounds in weight, which suggests determined fishing. The refuse-pit excavated on Iona shows that the diet was not always as ascetic as the monastic rules indicate, for the three hundred and four cattle joints which have been excavated, mostly prime cuts of beef with some haunches of venison, were hardly all consumed by guests. On Church Island (see p. 21), which appears to be a suitably remote site for ascetics, the monks were eating meat, fish and cereals. We should therefore beware of regarding the dietary prescriptions in the monastic Rules as universally applicable to the whole monastic population, for the Rules were probably written by enthusiasts during periods of reforming zeal. Asceticism was always possible, but excavation suggests that the diet in a monastic house was not very different from that in a lord's hall, except perhaps that fast seasons were observed more strictly.

The monks drank milk and whey, beer or water. Some ascetics refused to drink beer, but they were a minority, for even reformed ascetic communities were beer-drinkers. One conversation is reported between two *céli dé* leaders:

> 'The drink of forgetfulness of God shall not be drunk here', said the abbot of Tallaght.
>
> 'Well, my household shall drink it', replied the abbot of Finglas, 'and they will be in heaven along with your household.'

Even in ascetic communities beer must have been brewed for guests, and in the comfortable and satisfied guest the monastic poet saw the household of heaven at their drinking.

A monastery like the Skellig (see p. 19) may have supplied the inspiration for ascetics such as the hermit Paul whom Brendan visits in his Voyage, miraculously sustained on his rock by water and fish brought by a sea-otter. Presumably the monks on the Skellig imported sacks of meal or corn from the mainland, they must have fished and eaten the eggs of sea-birds, and they had a well and a small garden; but they could have done little cooking because there is no turf on the island, so for fire-wood they were presumably dependent on whatever wood the sea washed up. Such a life, followed by the whole community, was genuinely severe.

So the monastic diet varied, from house to house and within the monastery. Nor should we think that there was a regular monastic habit which all monks wore, as in a medieval Benedictine monastery. Normal early Irish aristocratic dress was a linen tunic with a leather belt, a woollen cloak fastened with a brooch, and leather shoes or boots, a costume which occurs constantly on the carved crosses and in manuscript illumination. The tunic was white, though it could be embroidered, and it could be worn long or short; the cloak was often in a bright colour, or at least with a bright border. On Muiredach's Cross at Monasterboice (Fig. 4) Christ is wearing a long tunic with a border and a cloak fastened by a brooch. Some people as early as the eighth century, probably the lower classes, were wearing jacket and trousers, a style found increasingly in the Viking Age: on Muiredach's Cross the soldiers arresting Christ are dressed in short breeches, and in a tenth-century Irish psalter now in the British Museum Goliath seems to be wearing trousers.

The dress of clerics as it appears on the stone carvings was a long tunic and a cloak: the literature shows that the colour varied according to the degree of austerity, the ascetics wearing a white tunic with little decoration and a cloak the colour of the natural wool. The Life of St Fintan tells how the king of Fotharta put out his two sons for fosterage in different religious establishments: when he went to visit them he found one wearing a hyacinth-coloured cloak with purple ornament and decorated shoes, the other in a dark cloak the colour of the sheep, a short white tunic with a black border, and common sandals. Of course in the story St Fintan persuades the king that the poorly clad son will be better off in the end, but in real life many aristocrats must have wanted their sons to be brought up in reasonable comfort. In *Hisperica Famina* the scholars wear nightgowns for sleeping, and in the morning put on linen tunics with leather belts and brown cloaks fastened with silver brooches; later in the composition they are said to be wearing purple and scarlet, with yellow caps on their curly yellow hair. Certainly the book-shrine of Maodhóg (*Breac Maodhóg* in the National Museum of Ireland) shows clerics and ladies with elaborate coiffures, long ringlets and beards arranged in different styles (Fig. 4). Just as the appearance of the rich and poor must have been very different, so the ascetic's dress and life-style contrasted with that of other clerics in the same monastery.

The work to be done was much the same as work on other

farms. The land had first to be prepared. One eighth-century tract classifies the land into six groups of varying value: best arable land, hilly arable land, land which has to be cleared but which is then fertile, 'land of ferny plains' which presumably was used for pasture, 'heathery mountain with furze on it', presumably suitable for sheep, and 'black land and bog' which

Fig. 4   Cleric from the *Breac Maodhóg* (metal shrine) and
Arrest scene from Muiredach's Cross at Monasterboice

provided turf for fuel. Ireland is a wet country, and agricultural land has to be properly drained: *Hisperica Famina* speaks of digging ditches. In windy places like the western plain of Iona which seems to be 'the harvest field', the corn needs protection, and here the seventh-century Life of Columba states that the monks built stone enclosures. Some aerial photographs show small fields surrounding monasteries, sometimes tiny, only a fraction of an acre. Such fields would probably be dug; but some monasteries

41

owned plough-teams, and there is some evidence which suggests that ploughing might be on a ridge-and-furrow principle, a system which implies a large open field. The Irish language has words for 'ridge' and 'furrow', and land might be measured in 'ridges': for instance, the King of Leinster gave Fiacc 'the fifth ridge of his father' on which to build Sleaty, which seems to mean the fifth 'strip' as the ridges and furrows would presumably be created by the method of ploughing. In the secular law tracts only the upper ranks of the aristocracy own a plough-team, the lower grades and the freemen own a half or quarter share of a plough (which may suggest that the plough team in early times was four oxen), while the unfree man has no such capital. The twelfth-century satire mentioned earlier speaks of eight different kinds of grain, and oats, barley, rye and wheat are all frequently referred to. The climate suits oats best of all, but barley seems also to have been popular, and wheat was the luxury grain. After it was harvested the corn had to be threshed, dried, ground and stored, so that a large monastery needed its own kiln, barns and water-mill, unless it was to grind the corn in hand-querns, a very arduous process. Quern stones have been found on some early monastic sites, and at Tallaght a small cross is set in a millstone. The saints' Lives mention all these processes: the plough oxen, sometimes in a team of six (*seisrech*), the iron ploughshares, the threshing and the grinding of the corn, which angels perform for specially favoured saints, and its storage in barns.

The stock was probably even more important than the arable farming, so fields had to be fenced, to keep animals in and to keep them out of the corn land. The secular laws emphasize the importance of fencing and the penalties for negligence; one eighth-century tract on neighbourhood defines the different kinds of fencing, the 'wall of three stones' (presumably in height), the fence made of wooden uprights, three bands of interwoven wicker and a crest of blackthorn. Fencing is one of the farm jobs which *Hisperica Famina* mentions, and when the master wishes to discourage a stupid student from further wasting his time and to send him back home, he tells him that his fields have broken gates, his cattle are grazing on the crops, his children are crying and his wife has gone to bed with another man.

The monastery needed horses for drawing carts and wagons and to give away as presents, for in a country without a coinage gifts were a necessary form of exchange, and a horse made a very acceptable gift. *Hisperica Famina* says that the horses were hobbled at night, and describes the herd of unbroken colts rolling and prancing and giving skittish looks at the passers-by. Oxen were kept for ploughing, the 'outer ox' being a specially well-trained animal who led the team. The monastery had its herds of cattle, important for their milk, their meat and their hides. The hides were used for a multitude of purposes; for boats, ropes, shoes, belts, harness, milk-vessels and cooking vessels, bed-coverings, book satchels and to make the vellum on which the books were written. Sheepskin could be used for many of the same functions: *Hisperica Famina* describes the manufacture of a book satchel out of sheepskin, the flaying of the animal and stret-ching and drying of the skin before the craftsman began his work on it, finishing it with a strap which the scholar could put round his neck or hang on a peg on the wall (Fig. 1). Iona had a special colony of seals on a small island off Mull ('the small island where the sea-calves which belong to us breed and are bred') which was worth raiding; the seal-skins must have been valuable.

There is far less in the saints' Lives about sheep than about cows, almost certainly because sheep were kept primarily for their wool and the processes of cloth manufacture were mainly women's work and were done at home, not in the monastery. The sheep of the early Celtic west was a small brown animal. It had first to be plucked or sheared. The wool then had to be teased and combed before it could be spun, all of which processes were performed by women, as the Irish law tracts show. The Romans had usually dyed their wool in the fleece before spinning it, and in Ireland the women made the dye: men might not be in the house while it was being manufactured. The law tracts speak of hand-weaving and loom-weaving: hand-weaving was a more primitive process, as the fines connected with its misuse are much less. After the cloth had been woven it had to be scoured to remove the natural grease, and fulled to shrink it and give it

43

greater density and a softer finish. The seventy-six fragments of cloth recovered from the royal lake-dwelling at Lagore make it possible to see the kind of weave and give some idea of the simple and narrow loom on which the cloth was woven. Flax was specially grown to make the linen needed for tunics, altar-cloths, and church hangings. Again it was the women who dried and spun the flax. Wool-fabric and linen manufacture were thus complicated processes, and a cloak in particular was a valuable article and a traditional form of payment.

Domestic arrangements are mentioned incidentally in the texts. A monastery usually had a kitchen separate from the refectory, and this was where the food was prepared. Meat had to be dried and salted. We know very little about how the Irish obtained their salt, though it was an essential commodity, and a lump of salt was an attractive present. It could have been obtained from sea-water by a process of evaporation, but there is some evidence that seaweed was collected and burned and the salty ashes used in curing meat. The monastic kitchen seems to have had no oven, and pottery is rare from excavated Irish sites except in the north-east. Dough for the bread was kneaded in wooden troughs and then baked on a griddle or baking flag, and bullauns (Fig. 21) which are often found on sites may have been used for grinding and preparing food (see p. 99). A cauldron, suitable for stews, was a luxury article, whilst meat might be roasted on spits or boiled in water heated by hot stones: clay pits or wooden vats could be used for this purpose. Vats made of staves bound with metal hoops have been found, possibly to take bath water, for the Irish liked to sit in their baths and it was only the ascetics who stood in cold water; the rest had their water heated with fire-stones kept for the purpose. Guests in particular were sometimes welcomed with a hot bath. All the same, the standard of cleanliness was not high: when the Irish geographer Dicuil, writing in 814, wanted to describe the summer solstice in Iceland, he said that it was light enough at night for the clerics to see to pick the lice out of their shirts. The monks slept in their own cells, though they sometimes shared cells, and although an ascetic might sleep on the bare ground with a stone for his pillow, other people in the monastery had couches with coverings. Literature, sculpture and illumination show us the monastic pets, the dogs and cats (Fig. 18) as well as some of the wild creatures which the hermits might tame.

Another essential commodity in the monastic economy was wood. Although many parts of Ireland now seem rather treeless, at this period Ireland was still well wooded, and a number of texts describe the cutting down and transport of trees, often a difficult task. *Hisperica Famina* describes how the trees which are to be felled are marked with knives, the roots chopped through with axes, and the trees felled, split with wedges and carried off in carts. On a windswept island like Iona where big trees do not grow the monks had to bring pine and oak trees from elsewhere, towing them with skiffs and curraghs through 'a long and devious route', praying the while for calm weather. One particular expedition provided timber to make a long-ship—the big wooden sea-going ship which was able to make long voyages and which differed from the curragh—a thin wooden frame covered with hides caulked at the seams which the monks normally used. Big timbers were also needed for building. On one occasion oak timbers were towed by twelve curraghs to Iona from the mouth of the river Sale (possibly the Shiel on the northern boundary of Argyllshire) for 'the renewing of the monastery'. In the Life of Brigit big trees are transported down a mountain-side by a miracle for the building of the church.

But wood was also needed for a host of smaller articles, for domestic furniture and equipment such as vats, butter-churns, for baskets of bark and brooms of twigs, for shingles with which to roof buildings (Fig. 7), for carts, for farm implements such as ox-yokes and for the major parts of instruments such as spades which were merely tipped with iron. Such things have survived in bogs or other waterlogged conditions. Wood was used also to make the scholar's writing-tablet described in *Hisperica Famina*, inlaid with wax, where the borders were decorated with carving 'fashioned with various painted designs'. A set of writing-tablets from Springmount Bog, Co. Antrim, probably dating from the seventh century, may be seen in the National Museum at Dublin. They comprise six leaves of yew wood, waxed and inscribed with

Fig. 5   Imaginative reconstruction of a tenth-century monastery
based on Nendrum

46

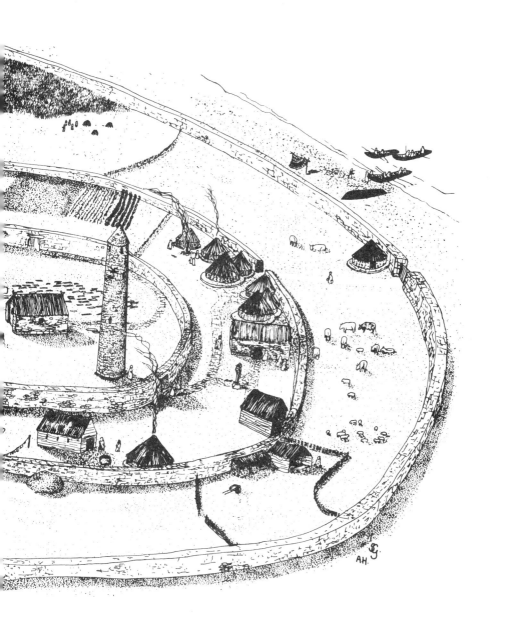

47

parts of two psalms, the whole held together with a leather strap. Wood was therefore necessary for the luxury articles as well as the basic necessities of life. There was plenty of it for burning, and while turf is now the normal fuel in the countryside, there are many references in the texts to the burning of wood in the early Irish period, both for domestic and industrial purposes.

The kind of economy I have described requires a lot of labour. At Iona the monks themselves did the farm work, and there seems to have been no distinction between choir monks and lay monks. In the seventh-century Life of Columcille we see the monks cultivating the fields on the west side of the island, land which during the 1939–45 war was used for farming. On Iona, it is the monks whom we see building the stone enclosures to protect the young crops from being blown away by gales, harvesting and carrying home the grain, milking the cows, towing the timbers in and erecting the buildings.

But this was not the universal custom, even at a very early period, for both canon and secular law speaks of the *manaig* ('monks'), the married laymen who lived with their wives and families and farmed the monastery's land. They probably lived outside the monastic enclosure, for just opposite Church Island (off Valencia) on Beginish there are fields with huts, which very probably housed the *manaig* who worked the fields which supplied the clerics on the island with the beef, oats and barley they were eating. Such people would come inside the monastic enclosure for protection in a time of crisis, they attended church on Sundays and partook of the host, as we see them doing in the Stowe Missal, and their eldest sons were educated in the monastic school and thus presumably became scholars and clerics.

A sizeable monastery also had its craftsmen and maintenance men, its smiths and builders and carpenters and boat-builders. One law tract (the Small Primer) says that the carpenter who can make an 'oak house' (*durthech*, the word often used for a timber church), the mill-wright, smith, woodcarver and ship-builder are all equal in status to the lowest of the noble grades of society, so they must have been well regarded in the monastery. At Clonmacnois there is a tombstone to a craftsman Tuathal (Fig.

16). The early law tracts show how important the mill was: it must have been, as Dr Lucas says, 'one of the commonest features of the countryside', complicated in its construction. Many of the monastic sites which have been excavated show traces of iron-working, slag and furnace-bottoms, and it seems likely that the tools used in the monastery, the ploughshares, sickles, spades, axes, knives, were all made on the spot: Adamnán's Life of Columba specifically refers to monks working the iron.

Big monasteries may have kept their own jewellers and fine metal-workers, or they may have employed them, for we hear in the texts of travelling craftsmen. Certainly they needed altar vessels and church equipment, patens and chalices, bells, croziers (Fig. 12), lamps and shrines. At Nendrum (Fig. 5) the excavators discovered huts where metal-working had gone on, finding moulds, unfinished pieces, crucibles, and tongs; but the equipment for making small objects of fine metal work was portable, and the craftsmen may have travelled. Certainly the styles of high crosses in different monasteries show some strong similarities, as if the stone-carvers moved around.

We should not imagine the scriptorium of a monastery as just a place where the writing and illumination was carried out. These were almost the final processes in a long series, followed by the careful checking over of the manuscript, necessary to ensure the transmission of a correct text. But before this stage was reached designs had to be tried out for illumination and metal work: we have a number of trial pieces in bone and stone, probably used before metal-working, or when a design was to be transferred from a manuscript to some other medium. The ink and pigments had to be prepared, and the preparation of the vellum, the calf-skin on which the manuscripts were written, was a major task. The Book of Kells, a very splendid Gospel-book, originally had about 370 folios measuring about $14\frac{1}{2} \times 10\frac{1}{4}$ ins; it is estimated that it needed about a hundred and fifty calves to produce this one book, and if only bull calves were killed the figure implies big herds and the collection of vellum over quite a long period, or its purchase. Book-production was both skilled and expensive. Books had to be bound, and the most important ones might even be enshrined.

The picture which I have drawn is of a large and prosperous monastery, but they were not all like this. We hear of foundations which failed, of monks who starved to death. There were bad times of cattle disease and famine and plague as the annals fairly frequently mention, when monasteries with small resources must have been especially badly hit; a long cold winter when pasture failed led to losses of cattle and pigs and sheep, and resulting shortage and disease. Yet what has been said must be true of a large number of those monasteries with long histories, whose ruins remain.

How was the monastery financed? The term is a misleading one, for the early Irish economy was without a coinage (though the Viking settlers used coins and started to mint their own shortly before 997). There is evidence that the original endowment was sometimes family land, and this may explain both why hereditary influence was strong, and why married laymen seem to have been settled on monastic lands from a very early period. There was an occasional income from bequest, for a man might bequeath what he had added to the family property by his own labour. Once set up, the monastery was economically an almost self-sufficient unit. It maintained people who did no manual work, the administrators, scholars, teachers, ascetics, but its *manaig* supplied the essential farm-labour force, for their land was monastic land and they paid a heavy rent in produce on it. It also had a regular income from fees for baptism and burial. If a boy of the secular free society came to the monastery for study he made an annual payment of a heifer, a pig, three sacks of malt and a sack of corn, with a milch-cow when he passed his first set of examinations, and a feast for five persons as the examiner's fee: so, at least, one tract states, and in the Life of Ciarán of Clonmacnois the young saint takes a cow to school with him whose 'hide remains to this day honourably in the city . . . and miracles are performed on it.' Some local small-trading transactions were made by exchange: for instance the monks of Iona fetched wattle for building a guest-house (from a layman,

50

presumably resident somewhere outside the island, because they fetched it by ship) in return for six measures of seed barley. Travelling craftsmen had to be paid—horses, cows, cloaks, brooches, and cauldrons are all cited as fairly frequent objects of exchange—so the monastery needed a surplus of such things as 'gifts'. A few expensive things had to be imported, chiefly wine and some dyes, which were presumably paid for in valuables or food-stuffs.

We can, therefore, build up a composite picture of the physical life of an early Irish monastery based on the written evidence, supplemented by archaeological material, imagining, let us say, a cleric travelling on foot to Clonmacnois from eastern Ireland, coming immediately from Durrow where he has just had a night's lodging. The time is afternoon in spring. As he reaches the end of the ridge-road he can see the fields stretched out round the monastery, the *manaig* and their helpers at work in them. Soon they will be driving home the cattle, penning up the sheep, herding the pigs into their sties, and hobbling the horses, before they themselves go home to their wives and children. The outer enclosure of the monastery is covered in dung, for there was a cattle raid in the vicinity yesterday and the stock was driven inside for safety: the steward has just heard that five cows were lost from an outlying pasture; 'Brief life, and hell hereafter' to the robbers. At the gate of the monastery the guest-master, who has seen the visitor approaching, comes to welcome him, and conducts him to the guest-house, where heated stones have already been put into the tub and a boy sent for meat and broth to the kitchen. The guest-house is well swept, with a comfortable fire and a cat lying before it, so the cleric takes off his cloak and, after his feet are washed, lets down his tunic which he had girded up for the journey. As he begins to eat, the bell rings for none and the monks, who have been sewing or reading in their separate huts, make their way over to the church. The guest-master explains that the abbot is away on circuit, but that the Master of the Schools will be delighted to see a visiting scholar. By the time the visitor has eaten and talked to the guest-master the service is over and the monks are in the refectory, where they are eating broth and bacon, bread and cheese, drinking beer, a boy playing to them on a little harp. In the school-house the boys are performing the nightly chores: some run to the woodpile for the fuel, some fetch water, others are cooking joints of meat and preparing the loaves, yet others making up the couches with leather covers. After the meal they have their homework to do by lamplight before they bank down the fire and go to bed. Dusk is falling in the small church, but one ascetic who has foregone the meal in the refectory is stretched out in prayer before the altar, while a solitary bird sings on the window-ledge. 'O Christ, O Christ, sever me not from thy sweetness.'

NOTE ON HISPERICA FAMINA

This text has been known for a long time, but the Latin is so difficult that few people have read it. It has recently been re-edited and translated by Michael Herren (*Hisperica Famina: 1. The A-Text*, Toronto 1974) and it is immediately obvious that if it describes a monastic milieu, it is excellent evidence for economy. It is early, written in the seventh century, relying heavily for its vocabulary on Isidore of Seville, a Spanish writer well known in Ireland. The various exercises intended to teach the pupils advanced Latin are based on the ordinary experiences of the student, the daily routine, the sky, the sea, the fire, the field, the wind, the book satchel, the writing-tablet, the church, prayer, and finally an attack by enemies on the settlement.

The recent editor tells me in conversation that he is confident, as I am, that the text comes from a monastic school. It certainly belongs to a Christian community. The tone and subject-matter are secular rather than pious, but this seems to me unimportant. The tenth-century Anglo-Saxon Aelfric wrote a grammar-book which deals mainly with comparable things in the Anglo-Saxon boys' experience, driving the sheep out to pasture, guarding them from wolves, ploughing, hunting, fishing, trading. These are not specifically religious occupations either, but Aelfric's book is undoubtedly for a monastic school. As I have already explained, an Irish monastery was a kind of 'city', not just a place of prayer for the religious. The *deversorius* (translated 'inn') which the students visit may be the house of the hospitaller (*briugu*) whose legal obligation it was to dispense hospitality. The 'protective walls of the town' to which they return are, I think, their own monastery, and here it is the *coloni* (? the *manaig*) who admit them and provide the food, though the students themselves cook it.

It is hard to believe that any of the vernacular schools of the 'poets' (*filid*) in the seventh century were using the very difficult and ornate Latin which the exercises aim to teach, whereas the familiarity of the monastic students with ordinary secular life need cause no surprise. We know that seventh-century canonists were experts in secular law, and that ecclesiastical writers knew well the conventions of the secular tales, so that the vestiges of pagan tradition which the editor sees in the text are explicable enough. I have therefore regarded *Hisperica Famina* as belonging to a monastic environment.

4

Buildings and other structures

The saints' Lives, annals and other written sources show us buildings of varying functions which once existed at early Irish monasteries, though how much remains of the early structures varies greatly from site to site. At Glendalough, for example, the beautiful valley is full of buildings—early churches, round tower, enclosure and cell—while at St Mullins, although we have a seventh-century plan of the monastery, most of the visible remains belong to the later medieval period. At many midland and eastern sites, where wood must long have been the most important building material, there is little early work to be seen, but in the west, in a landscape where stone is readily available, many sites are rich in standing remains.

The first thing to be seen may be the monastic enclosure. It is natural enough that it should be there: the enclosure provided a protective barrier, and farmsteads of the Early Christian period also had their surrounding banks and walls. But excavation suggests that the elaborate enclosures of some secular forts do not necessarily imply conditions of extreme violence; they were, rather, status symbols, for in the law tracts a man's status is indicated by the size of his stockade, and an important monastery would have been able to call on large labour resources for building an enclosure. The circuit also delineated the legal area belonging to the monastery which was regarded as holy (the *termon*) and was to be free from aggression. Some ascetics evidently saw the enclosure as shutting out the world, probably rather unsuccessfully unless, as we know sometimes happened, the ascetics occupied a separate enclosure within the main one or at a distance from it. Whether or not the circuit is still clear at a site, we can be sure that it did exist and that it played an important part in the life of the monastery.

The enclosure could have been defined by earthen banks and

ditches, stone walls, timber, wattles or even thorn bushes. We can hardly expect to see those made of perishable materials, like the circular withy hedge which Giraldus the Welshman saw at Kildare late in the twelfth century. But stone walls are visible at many sites, for example at Glendalough which has an imposing arched gateway, at Mayo, Nendrum, and numerous western coastal and island monasteries. Earthworks are perhaps less obvious, but there is an impressive and extensive complex of earthen banks around the church at Seirkieran, where the graveyard occupies only a very small part of the large enclosure. In making for the obvious focus, usually a church or graveyard, it is easy to cross the enclosure without realizing it, but it is worth looking from the graveyard for traces of banks, walls, hedges or lanes on the line of the original circuit.

The observer at ground level, however, even in the best conditions of low-level sunlight and little vegetation, only sees part of the picture, and recently the search for monastic enclosures has been spectacularly aided by air photography. The aerial camera, from its high-level view-point, takes in a large area with little or no distortion from perspective, and it can pick out subtle variations in soil, crop colour and height, and shadow resulting from differences in relief. A picture, fragmentary, confused and distorted to the ground-level observer, becomes more complete, clearer, and more intelligible from the air. Rivers and streams, curving hedges, roads and lanes, banks and ditches and walls, all these, seen from the air, can provide clues to the line of the monastic enclosure. At the great monastery of Clonard, for example, there is little to see except the Protestant church in its graveyard, but from the air the church is seen to be within a circular enclosure, and the adjoining fields are full of slight earthworks suggesting intensive activity in the area.

There were large and small monasteries, and large and small enclosures, from about 100 feet (or even less) to 600 feet and more in diameter. A roughly circular or oval outline was common, although D-shaped and sub-rectangular examples are known. There may have been a single circuit, or two or three concentric rings as at Nendrum (Fig. 5). The interesting concentric street plan at Armagh suggests a former double, if not triple, enclosure around the hilltop, and excavation has discovered a stretch of ditch south of the cathedral. At Killabuonia (Fig. 6) the buildings are arranged on three terraces, and here the stone walls which revet the hillside must have performed the function of the enclosure walls elsewhere. Sometimes there are more extensive and complex enclosures and earthworks, as at Ardpatrick (Limerick), on Inishcaltra, and round the two churches at Liathmore. Within the main enclosure are sometimes traces of subdivisions. At Kildrenagh (Loher) and other Kerry sites the

Fig. 6   Killabuonia upper terrace showing cell (left)
tomb (centre) and ruined church (upper right)

church and graveyard are divided from the rest of the enclosure by a wall. There are four divisions within the wall at Inishmurray, and subdivisions can be traced at Inchcleraun, Kiltiernan, Moyne and elsewhere. Such internal divisions could define areas of differing degrees of sanctity which early legislation speaks of, and areas for specialized activities, such as worship, housing for clerics and ascetics, education, crafts and hospitality. This is a question which excavation could help to answer.

Many graveyards at early monastic sites have a distinctively rounded outline and with long use have become greatly raised above their surroundings. Sometimes a raised, roughly circular

nucleus is visible in a larger graveyard, distinguished by a cluster-
ing of older graves. Some of these round cemeteries may reflect
the shape of an early monastic enclosure, though the original
enclosure must often have been much bigger than the present
graveyard. Circular cemeteries occur widely in western Britain as
well as Ireland, but this is not a well-studied or well-understood
phenomenon.

Within the enclosure the focal point of the monastery was the
church. We must recognize at the outset that early Irish churches
are very difficult to date, and there are uncertainties and conflict-
ing statements in different sources. One view is that stone
churches were being built well before the Viking invasions and
that surviving ruins extend from perhaps the seventh to the
twelfth century. But it can also be argued that stone building was
for long exotic in Ireland, and whilst some stone churches were
being built at important monasteries in the tenth and eleventh
centuries, many sites may not have had their first stone church
until the twelfth century or even later. Why is it so difficult to
suggest a chronology for the earliest Irish stone churches?
Buildings are most satisfactorily dated by inscriptions on the
fabric or written sources which refer to the surviving building.
More loosely, they can be dated by typology and analogy: that is,
by establishing a sequence of plans, details of doors, windows,
decoration and so on, observing when these occur in datable
buildings, and transferring the dates (cautiously) to other structures exhibiting the same features. The chronology of pre-
Norman churches in Anglo-Saxon England is not easy to establish, yet there are more fixed points than in Ireland, where the
earliest certainly datable churches belong to the twelfth century.
The Irish churches are very simple, lacking closely datable
features; inscriptions are rare and written sources give little help
in dating particular structures. The problem is vividly illustrated
by the widely diverging dates, ranging from the seventh to the
twelfth century, which are ascribed to the best-known 'early'
Irish church, Gallarus oratory.

We can introduce the traveller to these problems, but hardly
rehearse the arguments in all their detail. It is, however, clear that

the traditional Irish method of building was in wood. Bede recognized this in the early eighth century and contrasted it with the 'Roman' tradition of stone and mortar building practised in Anglo-Saxon England. Wooden building was still regarded as the traditional Irish method as late as the twelfth century, and when St Malachy restored the monastery of Bangor he constructed an oratory 'made of smoothed planks, closely and strongly fastened together' in what his biographer, St Bernard of Clairvaux, described as 'an Irish fashion'. The waterlogged wood excavated from lake settlements (crannogs) gives us some idea of the high standard of carpentry in early Ireland—the carefully shaped structural members with mortice and tenon joints and beautifully turned wooden vessels and utensils. Whatever the date of the earliest stone churches—and I incline towards the later date-range—we must visualize lost centuries of accomplished building in wood, and so it is to timber churches that we must turn our attention first.

Written sources allow us glimpses of wooden churches. *Hisperica Famina* (see p. 52) describes what seemed to the seventh-century writer to be a 'massive' wooden church, with a vaulted roof, four *pinnae* (translated by the editor as 'steeples', but perhaps in fact something smaller than this word suggests), one door in the west end and a plank-built *porticus* (which in contemporary Anglo-Saxon churches meant a side-chapel). Another text usually ascribed to the seventh century, Cogitosus's Life of Brigit, gives an account of a church recently rebuilt at Kildare—an unusual church since it had to provide for nuns and clerics as well as the laity. Here the east end was divided from the rest of the church by a screen, and another screen ran down the centre of the church to the west end; the priests and laymen entered by a door on the south side, and the women by a door on the north side. This seems to be a different plan from the early stone churches (Fig. 8), which always have a west door, and these two descriptions make us wary about assuming very standardized plans for seventh-century timber churches. At Kildare, difficulty arose over the rebuilding, for they re-hung the ancient north door, and it needed a miracle to make it close satisfactorily. Saints' Lives often refer to 'fair-boarded' churches of smooth planks, some of them large ones; wooden shingles or thatch formed the roof, and the floor may have been strewn with reeds or straw.

Excavation provides a more detailed view of particular sites. Traces of wooden post-hole structures have been found underneath stone churches on sites as widely separated as Church Island (off Valencia), Ardagh (Longford) and White Island, as well as in Scotland and Wales, but more excavation is needed to

Book of Kells

Muiredach's Cross, Monasterboice: Finial

Fig. 7   Timber churches

build up a fuller picture. The stone finials of some tenth-century high crosses may allow another glimpse of these lost wooden churches (Fig. 7). At Durrow, Monasterboice and elsewhere, the finial seems to be modelled on a house- or oratory-shaped shrine which may, in turn, preserve some features of timber building like the shingled roof and the winged finials at the ends of the roof-ridge.

Though the early Irish normally built in wood, they were certainly not unfamiliar with stone churches. Always great travellers, Irish churchmen had plenty of opportunities to see stone

59

churches, in seventh-century Northumbria, for example, in Merovingian Gaul or in the Carolingian empire in the ninth century and later, and in the twelfth when St Malachy built a stone church at Bangor, following the pattern of 'those which he had seen constructed in other regions'. If they adhered largely to timber building until the eleventh and twelfth centuries it was not through ignorance, but by choice and tradition. It is possible, therefore, that many of the simple stone churches that survive on early Irish ecclesiastical sites are no earlier than the eleventh and twelfth centuries. They can be safely, if rather broadly, described as pre-Romanesque, showing none of the characteristics of that style.

They have distinctive features. Most surviving early Irish churches are small, though a few larger ones exist, like the 'cathedral' at Glendalough, to remind us of the bigger churches at important sites which must once have existed. In their day these must have been imposing and influential structures, and they are the archaeologists' 'missing links'. The surviving small churches (sometimes as small as 7 by 8 feet or 7 by 10½ feet) are commonly simple and box-like, a rectangle without porches, aisles, sacristies, towers or other elaborations of plan or elevation (Fig. 8). The door is always at the west end, and when it is not, there may well be traces of a blocked west door or evidence that the north or south one is inserted, as at Temple Cronan (Fig. 8) and Dulane. The door-jambs usually incline inwards slightly, and the lintel (the stone above the door) is often very large, with a second relieving lintel sometimes set above the main one to spread the weight. Doors can be elaborated slightly with an architrave (a projecting moulding outlining the opening, seen in Fig. 13) and very occasionally there is a carved cross on or above the lintel. Projecting pierced stones sometimes visible just inside the door must have held the door-frame. Windows were usually few and small, with a rounded, triangular or flat head, and interiors must have been very dark.

A common feature, peculiar to Irish churches, is *antae*, that is, the projecting of the side walls slightly beyond the line of the gable walls to east and west (Temple MacDuagh in Fig. 8). *Antae* are unlikely to be structural buttresses, as there is no particular thrust at this point, but they may echo timber construction,

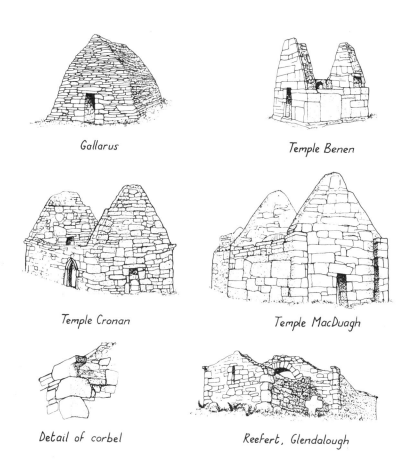

Gallarus

Temple Benen

Temple Cronan

Temple MacDuagh

Detail of corbel

Reefert, Glendalough

Fig. 8   Stone churches

representing angle posts projecting beyond the plank walls. In stone churches *antae* could have supported timbers, known as barge boards, which in turn protected the exposed ends of the roof members. The same function was sometimes performed by a pair of projecting corbels at eaves level, as at Temple Cronan and Reefert church, Glendalough (Fig. 8). From an aesthetic point of view *antae* lend some vertical emphasis to an otherwise largely featureless elevation, and in sunshine introduce an attractive element of contrasting light and shade, absent from perfectly flat surfaces.

The stonework of these churches deserves close attention and it varies greatly from area to area according to local supplies (Figs 8 and 11). In County Clare and the Aran Islands, for example, huge thin limestone slabs were set on edge enclosing a rubble core, giving the wall the appearance of massive solidarity (Temple Benen in Fig. 8). In other areas large polygonal stones were carefully fitted together and the spaces between plugged with small stones (known as spalls or pinnings). In areas of slabby shale and slate, like County Down, walls were sometimes built of carefully laid, thin slabs. Granite walls tend to look less tidy, with much use of irregularly sized boulders (Fig. 11), but jambs and quoins are often large pieces of carefully hammer-dressed granite. The standard of stonework and the care taken in fitting the stones together is often noticeably higher than in medieval and post-medieval churches in the particular area, an interesting reflection on Early Christian craftsmanship. Some of these early churches are built without mortar, some clearly with mortar, and in other cases modern repointing makes it difficult to be sure.

Thatch and shingles must be imagined for roofing, and the very steep pitch of some surviving gables would be good for draining these perishable materials. But a few early stone churches had all-stone roofs, like Gallarus oratory (Figs 8 and 9). This remarkable little building is almost complete and gives an idea of the small, high, dark interior of many pre-Romanesque churches. Its walls are corbelled, each stone projecting a little inwards beyond the one below and sloping slightly outwards and downwards to throw off water, so ascending in a gentle curve to the ridge. The west door has sloping jambs and a relieving lintel, and the single small east window is round-headed. Oratories of this kind are confined to Kerry and other western coastal counties, geographically on the fringe, away from the great monastic centres of Armagh, Clonmacnois, Clonard, Kildare and Lismore. They must not be thought of as the 'typical' early Irish church,

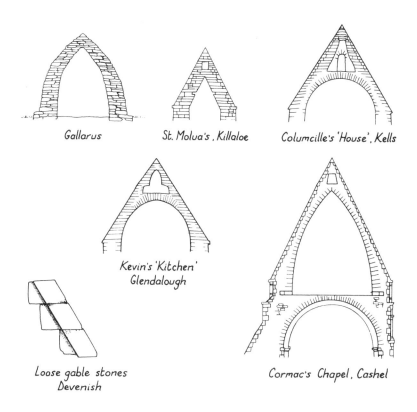

Fig. 9   Sections through stone-roofed churches

and there is no reason to regard them as earlier than 'early' stone churches elsewhere in Ireland, though their dating remains a matter of some controversy.

The stone-roofed church, though rare compared with wooden and thatch roofs, was an Irish speciality (Fig. 9); indeed one could call it an Irish eccentricity, since it involves a great deal of labour and imposes a very heavy burden on the walls. In more sophisticated structures than the corbelled oratories each roofing stone was cut to the shape of the roof and flat bedded on the stone below. The roof might be freestanding or have internal timber supports, as on St MacDara's Island or at St Molua's church from Friar's Island at Killaloe; others had a small croft or attic room above a stone arch, which propped up the stone roof, as at Kevin's 'Kitchen', Glendalough, and Columcille's 'House' at Kells. Some of the roofs still stand, but others have collapsed under the heavy load: St Molaise's 'House' on Devenish, for example, which old drawings and loose stones (Fig. 9) show was of this type, is reduced to its low foundations.

The most highly developed of the stone-roofed churches is Cormac's Chapel, Cashel, which is in a fully Romanesque tradition (Fig. 11 shows a detail of its sandstone masonry). Distinctively Romanesque work will be found at many early monastic sites, so it must be briefly mentioned, though it is not possible to deal with it in detail here. H. G. Leask suggested a time-span for Irish Romanesque from the late eleventh century to about 1200, but Mr de Paor has more recently argued convincingly that Cormac's Chapel at Cashel, dedicated in 1134, marks the beginning. Two-cell, nave and chancel, plans became more common in the twelfth century, as at the Nuns' Church and Temple Finghin at Clonmacnois, and the churches at Rahan and Monaincha. But the main impact was not on plan but on decoration, lavished especially richly on doors and chancel arches. Irish craftsmen have always delighted in exploiting the decorative potential of new styles, whilst impressing on the borrowings their own peculiar stamp, and so we find *antae* persisting, and west doors with sloping jambs, as at Clonfert, Kilmalkedar (Fig. 10) and Roscrea, but also the rich, deeply undercut, three-dimensional decoration characteristic of the later twelfth century in England.

Early Irish churches have often undergone much alteration, and it is instructive to look for signs of additions and subtractions, changes in masonry, straight joints, and blocked or altered openings (Fig. 11). When a pre-Romanesque or Romanesque church has a chancel, it is worth looking carefully to see whether the chancel has been added. A few early churches were two-celled from the first, like Trinity and Reefert churches at Glendalough (Reefert is seen in Fig. 8); but often the chancel has clearly been

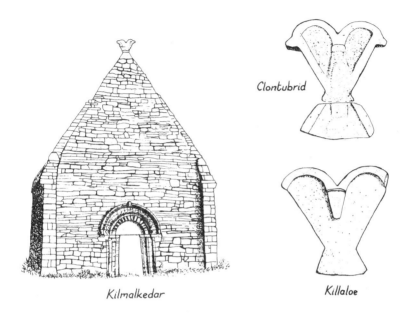

Clontubrid

Kilmalkedar

Killaloe

Fig. 10   A Romanesque west front with *antae*,
finial and door with sloping jambs,
and two loose finials

added, sometimes tucked in between the eastern *antae* as at Tullaherin (Fig. 11), or built as an extension of the *antae* as at Maghera (Derry). In a few cases, part or all of an early church has been swallowed up in a greatly enlarged building, and it is possible to see the different masonry, as at Ardfert (Fig. 11) and Ardmore, or the line of the original gable, as at Drumacoo, Temple Brecan and Temple Doolin at Clonmacnois (Fig. 11). Later medieval changes often included a change in the position of

65

the door and alterations to windows. Worked stones lying loose in a graveyard or built into a wall may also provide clues to a building now vanished or much altered: the loose gable finial at Killaloe cathedral or the one built into a well-house at Clontubrid near Freshford must once have crowned gable tops as at

Tullaherin   Kiltiernan   Clonmacnois
                              Temple Doolin

Ardfert Cathedral   Castledermot   Cashel
                         (granite)   (sandstone ashlar)

Fig. 11   Alterations to churches and types of masonry

Kilmalkedar (Fig. 10). Long stones may have been the lintels of doors, like the stone decorated with a Crucifixion scene at Dunshaughlin, and small, loose, semi-circular window-heads will sometimes be recognized. Such stones, detached from their original context, may at first puzzle the observer, but they are clues to structures now altered, badly ruined or entirely disap-peared—further pieces in the intricate jigsaw of reconstruction.

Architectural detective work of this kind can be very exciting, and one detailed example will show how close observation can disentangle the structural history of a church. On Inishmacsaint in Lower Lough Erne is a ruined church, long and narrow with a south door and no structural division between nave and chancel. The west wall is about twenty-four feet long, and the side walls for thirty-six feet eastwards stand on a neat cut stone foundation, whilst the rest of the north and south walls and the east wall stand on a quite different foundation of large, irregularly shaped stones. Close observation suggests that a patch of different masonry in the middle of the west wall marks the position of a blocked door, and the south door is clearly an insertion. The conclusion must be that we have a small, pre-Romanesque church, 24 × 36 feet, with the usual west door, altered and extended eastwards (in this case probably in about 1200) to form the long, narrow rectangle we now see.

How were these early churches used? The surviving fabric provides some clues, and the written sources help us to imagine their furnishing and equipment. In the new church at Kildare, the tombs of Brigit and Conlaeth, the first bishop, were on either side of the altar, adorned with gold and silver and precious stones, with gold and silver crowns hanging above them. The transverse screen was decorated with paintings and linen curtains. One of the churches visited by Brendan on his Voyage had three altars, the central one with three lamps, the side altars each with two hanging lamps, with candles placed inside them: perhaps this is a reference to the fine 'hanging bowls' whose purpose has puzzled the archaeologists, but which could have acted as reflec-tors. There were twenty-four seats in this church for the monks, presumably down each side as in a modern college chapel, for the abbot led the singing and the monks chanted antiphonally, ans-wering each other from side to side. Elsewhere we find a refer-ence to fourteen seats opposite each other, with the abbot's seat placed centrally, the kind of seating arrangement which is shown in the Temptation scene in the Book of Kells (Fig. 7), where the timber church has gable finials and a shingled roof, and the monks are facing each other.

Large churches must have been used for congregational worship: the church at Derry where neighbouring lay people took refuge in the late sixth century cannot have been very small, nor the church at Trevet, where the annals tell us that 140 people were burned in 1120. An early eighth-century text indicates that two churches at Armagh were used by different groups—bishops, priests and anchorites in one, and virgins, penitents and *manaig* in the other. But many of the tiny surviving churches were clearly not for congregational worship on any scale. The smallest would not have held more than half a dozen people, hardly even the twelve envisaged in the ninth-century 'Hermit's Song':

> Four times three, three times four, fit for every need,
> Twice six in church, both north and south.

Some small churches were clearly over or close to particular burials, such as St Declan's 'House' at Ardmore and Temple Ciaran at Clonmacnois, and pilgrims must have resorted there, and mass would have been said by a priest in them. Early altars do not very commonly survive, but on Inishmurray a stone altar contains a cavity which must have held relics, and some 'relic altars' have been excavated in western Britain.

A distinctive feature of early Irish monasteries is the multiplication of small churches. The legendary seven is not common, but clusters of churches can be seen at many sites including Ardfert, Clonmacnois (Fig. 22), Glendalough, Inishcaltra, Inchcleraun and Temple Brecan on Inishmore. It seems to have been the practice often to build another small church rather than rebuild or enlarge an existing one. The view of a cluster of many roofless small churches, often of widely differing dates, as at Kilmacduagh, is a peculiarly Irish one. At several sites a church is set apart from the main group of buildings and is associated with women. There is the Nuns' Church at Clonmacnois, St Mary's at Glendalough (which few of Glendalough's many visitors seem to see), and the Women's Churches at Inchcleraun, Inishglora and Inishmurray. At Lemanaghan a rewarding walk is from the ruined Romanesque church, south-eastwards along a stone causeway through the marsh, to a neglected small early church in a badly overgrown enclosure, traditionally the cell of St Manchán's mother, perhaps another 'women's church'.

Although surviving early Irish churches are small and simple and lack architectural subtleties, they have their own modest qualities and hold a particular fascination for those who do not demand grandeur of scale and elaboration of plan and elevation. But some mental effort is needed to re-roof them, furnish their bare interiors, and restore the succession of their 'fair-boarded' wooden predecessors.

Another important building within the monastic enclosure at many sites was a round tower (Fig. 12), usually standing close to the church (often a little to the north-west). This is the most striking feature of many monasteries, summoning the traveller from miles away, and it is often the earliest surviving building. 'No towers are more graceful than these upward-pointing stone fingers of Ireland' (Conant), and they are indeed an impressive architectural achievement for a people whose building traditions were grounded in timber construction. At least 120 round towers were recorded in the nineteenth century and others are known from written sources. Some have disappeared in quite recent times: there is an eighteenth-century drawing of Downpatrick tower, now vanished; Killeshin tower was demolished in 1703 because a farmer was afraid that it would fall on his cows; the top of Maghera (Down) tower fell early in the eighteenth century and is said to have lain intact on the ground like a huge gun-barrel. Recently excavation has brought two 'new' and unsuspected towers to light at Liathmore and Devenish, and further examples may still be uncovered. The standing remains range from complete towers, like those at Kilmacdaugh and Glendalough, to low foundations like the stumps at Nendrum (Fig. 12) and St Mullins. At Cashel the tower was joined to the cathedral's north transept in the thirteenth century, whilst at Lusk it was used as one angle turret of the fine late medieval parish church tower, and three other circular turrets were built to match it.

69

Round towers are tall and slender, ranging from about 70 to 120 feet high, tapering gradually and gracefully upwards, and finishing (when intact) in a conical cap. The top has, however,

Nendrum   Drumcliff   Kilmacduagh   Kildare

Fig. 12   Round towers, ruined, intact and altered,
with the Lough Lene Bell and the Bann crozier

often suffered from lightning or decay: some are rebuilt in the original form, some rebuilt with a different top, like the crenellated parapets at Cloyne and Kildare (Fig. 12), and others remain ruined. The masonry ranges from unworked rubble to carefully cut and fitted ashlar (dressed stone), and a number of towers show several contrasting types of stonework, which may indicate

rebuildings, for example at Kildare and Timahoe, but this phenomenon has not yet been studied in detail. At Roscam, holes in
the masonry for wooden scaffolding can be seen. The door is
characteristically high above the ground (though the ground level
has often changed) and can only have been reached by a movable
ladder. There may be signs of how the door was fitted inside. The
door opening (Fig. 13) may have a flat lintelled head or a semi-
circular one, either cut from a single stone or made up of
individually shaped stones, and the opening is often outlined with
a slightly projecting architrave. Windows are usually few and

Fig. 13   Round tower doors

small, commonly flat-headed but sometimes with a triangular
head, and there are often four windows just below the cap. Only a
few towers have any decoration, for example a crucifixion above
the lintel at Donaghmore (Meath) and a cross at Antrim (Fig. 13),
spirals on the architrave at Rattoo (Fig. 13), elaborate
Romanesque doors at Kildare and Timahoe (Fig. 13), and a
cornice decorated with heads around the base of the cap at
Devenish. When the internal arrangements can be traced, it is
clear that there were wooden floors: some had four or five, but
others six, seven or even eight. The floors were supported by
joists resting either in holes or on ledges contrived in the wall

thickness. Access must have been by ladders from floor to floor: the admittedly rather laborious climb up Monasterboice tower shows something like the original arrangement.

Round towers were the subject of fierce and eccentric debate in the nineteenth century, when even their ecclesiastical nature was in doubt: they were claimed as, amongst other things, Buddhist temples, penitential prisons, phallic symbols and stylite columns. But the great antiquary George Petrie settled their context and function beyond doubt in the book published in 1845, *The Ecclesiastical Architecture of Ireland*. They are peculiar to church sites, and even if no church is visible, as at Antrim, there will usually be some record of its former existence. They served as belfries, as their Irish name *cloictheach* suggests, but they had other uses, especially the safe-keeping of people and treasures. The round tower of Slane was being used as a place of safety in 950 when it was burned by the Vikings of Dublin: 'The crozier of the patron saint, and a bell that was the best of bells, Caenechair, the Man of Learning [and] a multitude along with him were burned'. (Fig. 12 shows a bell and crozier.) The idea was presumably to shepherd people and treasures into the tower in the hope of sitting out an attack, but here the outer stone shell failed to prevent a disastrous fire, and internally, chimney-like and wooden, these towers must have been horribly combustible. In more peaceful times the hand-bell for services would be rung from the top windows, perhaps from each in turn, north, south, east and west. Towers would admittedly have attracted attention to monasteries, as they still do, unwelcome in Viking context, but perhaps a symbol in peaceful times, like the spires which were so popular in thirteenth- and fourteenth-century England.

When were round towers first built? Petrie believed that some belonged to the time of the great monastic founders in the sixth and seventh centuries, and some might still argue for an early date. But their first appearance in the annals is the Slane reference in 950, and they were still being built in the twelfth and thirteenth centuries: the decoration at Devenish, Kildare and Timahoe suggests a twelfth-century date, and the fine tower at Ardmore cannot be far from 1200. The problem of dating is tied up with the question of origins. Round towers of this kind are peculiar to Ireland, not quite like anything anywhere else, except for two in Scotland. Their oddity lies in their very tall, thin proportions and their freestanding situation. Italian *campanili* are freestanding but very different in shape and proportions. Much more like the Irish towers are the tall, thin staircase turrets common in French and German churches in the ninth, tenth and eleventh centuries. Irish monks were prominent among the scholars at the court of Charlemagne and his successors and had plenty of opportunities for observing models. It is in this milieu that I believe the origins of the round towers in Ireland are to be sought, and if this is so, we must see them originating immediately following the period of the worst Viking attacks on Ireland, in the late ninth or early tenth century, and perhaps at those sites most vulnerable to attack. But by the eleventh century, when written references to towers increase greatly, the Viking menace had passed. Defensive considerations doubtless receded and others—emulation, prestige, symbolism—became more prominent.

Written sources indicate a wide range of other structures, and at some sites other buildings are visible besides the church and round tower, but it is not always easy to tie together the written sources and material evidence and suggest functions for the buildings. One point is, however, very clear from sites like Inishmurray, Killabuonia and Nendrum: the planning of early Irish monasteries was irregular (Fig. 5). There may have been some zoning of different activities in particular areas, but there is no hint of the regular lay-out of buildings around a cloister which had certainly appeared in England by the tenth century and perhaps earlier. At a medieval monastery the visitor quickly becomes familiar with the orderly, almost stereotyped, arrangement of buildings round the cloister—the chapter-house, dormitory, refectory and so on. In early Irish monasteries we are in a different world, and to appreciate the contrast fully it is illuminating to go from Monasterboice to Cistercian Mellifont, from Nendrum to Grey Abbey or Inch, both Cistercian abbeys not far away, or from Kilree to the Augustinian priory at Kells (Kilkenny) nearby.

73

A second area of contrast is in the different provision of private and communal accommodation. Benedictine monasticism emphasized the discipline of communal life, in the shared dormitory, dining-room, warming-house and working-room. Early Irish monasteries had certain communal rooms but there was much more emphasis on individual practice and observance, and so we can look for a contrast between individually and communally used buildings.

Most important among the former were the living-cells, occupied by clerics singly or in twos and threes. The abbot's house

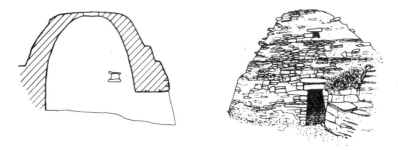

Fig. 14   Skellig Michael, cell A

is prominent in written sources: in 975, for example, the abbot of Nendrum was burned 'in his own house'. A Life of Monenna describes how she would spend all day shut in her cell at prayer, and Columcille had his own cell on Iona where he used to write. It is only in the stony west that cells (Fig. 14) survive at all commonly, and they are best seen on Skellig Michael, and on other island and coastal sites like Illauntannig, Inishkea, Inishmurray and Killabuonia. They are roughly circular corbelled stone structures—*clocháns*—built in the same way as Gallarus oratory, and there is evidence that they may sometimes have been surrounded by a turf covering, presumably to help in weather-proofing. When they survive intact they are dark but still dry and surprisingly spacious: at Skellig Michael cell A is about 16 feet across and 16 feet high, and cell C is $9\frac{1}{2}$ feet across and 12 feet high. Wall cupboards are provided. At Church Island (off Valencia) excavation showed that a circular stone hut had, like the church, been preceded by a wooden structure, and in the less stony midlands and east the living-cells must often have been built of wood, but these will only be found by excavation.

Apart from the church the most important communal building was the refectory, for it seems that the monks usually ate together. The kitchen must have been close by: Columbanus's Rule forbade monks to visit the kitchen after none. The excavator would hope for signs of fires, and perhaps burned stones, since food was boiled by heating water with hot stones, and there should be middens with food refuse not far away (see pages 36–48).

The guesthouse is prominent in written sources (see page 14). St Molua's first care when building a monastery was said to be provision for visitors, and a Rule insisted on 'a clean house for guests and a big fire, washing and bathing for them, and a couch without sorrow'. Saints' Lives suggest that the guesthouse was sometimes set away from the main monastic buildings, and when a monastery is excavated on a big enough scale to see the relationship of buildings to one another, the guesthouse is likely to stand somewhat apart.

We occasionally hear of sick monks, but there is little mention of infirmaries specially devoted to the sick. Perhaps we should visualize care in individual cells, more feasible than in the communal dormitories of a later medieval monastery. One of the buildings at Nendrum was called 'the school' by its excavator, but it may not be necessary to envisage a distinct, recognizable building for this purpose except at major sites. The impression given by (admittedly late) Lives is of instruction given in the cell, in the open air, wherever the master was, though in *Hisperica Famina* (see p. 52) there seems to be a special house where the schoolboys lived. And should we necessarily imagine a distinct scriptorium except at important sites? The Nendrum 'school' is best regarded as the workshop where various specialized crafts were practised, for the finds included stones with scratched trial designs, styluses, knives, needles, and a small mortar, perhaps for crushing pigments. One of the circular hut foundations nearby produced crucibles, moulds, and tongs and was probably used for bronze-working. An excavated round hut at Ballyvourney had been used for iron-working (though the excavation did not establish that the context was certainly monastic) and evidence of dyeing was found on Inishkea North. There must have been a range of agricultural and domestic buildings associated with a monastery, though not necessarily in the main enclosure—barns, byres, stables, sheds, stores, kilns, mills and brew-houses. Buildings of this kind are occasionally mentioned in written sources, but some may have been fairly slight in construction, like some modern sheds, and would thus have left little trace.

It must be recognized that the traveller is rarely going to be able to assign a specialized function to a particular building: he will usually have to be content with the rather general term 'cell'. At important sites—'great' Armagh and Clonmacnois, 'multitudinous' Devenish, Glendalough and Kildare, 'mighty' Ferns and all others—he must imagine a large population and a wide range of activities and buildings. At smaller sites, on the other hand, it is probably not appropriate to visualize such a range of activities and of specialized, functionally distinct buildings: prayer, meditation, reading, writing, instruction, crafts, none of these demands particularly elaborate accommodation. Gradually excavation may make it possible to distinguish between individually and communally used structures and to detect functional differences between buildings.

A feature present at many church sites, though not always easy to see, is a souterrain. They are reported at Donaghmore (Down), Glencolumbkille, Killala, Kiltiernan, Kildreelig and elsewhere. As the name suggests, these are underground structures, similar to Cornish fogous and Scottish earth-houses. The usual form is a dry-stone passage built in a trench, roofed with large flat slabs and covered with earth. They can be cut from solid rock, but this is laborious and less common. There may be a single passage, but sometimes the plan is more complex with branches, chambers and changes of level. Souterrains occur fairly commonly in secular settlements of the Early Christian period and probably total thousands over all Ireland, but no count has yet been made. It is fairly widely agreed that they were constructed primarily for storage, to provide a cool, dry, secure store for perishable food-stuffs, which secular and ecclesiastical communities alike would need to keep. But in some cases defensive considerations were probably also present: there are sometimes well-concealed secret passages and highly inconvenient constrictions and changes of level in the passage. It is always difficult to assess people's toler-ance of discomfort in the past, but who would choose to squeeze through a gap only 1 foot 6 inches by 2 feet 6 inches on the way to fetch butter? We should probably regard these structures as cellars where people might occasionally take temporary refuge with their valuables. By their nature souterrains are not usually easy to see unless ruined and collapsed, and the entrance is not commonly left open. If a visitor encounters an open one he should not venture down it without good light, and he should check that it is safe before embarking on any exploration.

Close to the church was the graveyard, and a specially impor-tant grave formed the focal point of many cemeteries (Fig. 6). The relics of the founder or a revered saint brought great spir-itual and material rewards to a monastery. The remains could be in the church, as we have seen, but if they were outside, they would be marked in a special way, and it is sometimes possible still to distinguish this focus. There may be simply a cross-carved stone, like the slab north of the church at Kildreelig, or a more complicated structure, like the mound known as St Cummin's tomb at Kilcummin, which has two pillars at the ends and a cross-carved slab between. Small rectangular enclosures, defined by upright stone kerbing and often called saints' 'beds' (*leabai*). may cover special graves: people are said to have slept in *Leaba Bhreacáin* at Temple Brecan as a sign of gratitude if their prayers for recovery from illness were answered.

A simple but distinctive kind of special grave was a tent-shaped stone shrine, probably designed to hold exhumed bones. Two large slabs incline and meet at the ridge and are closed by two triangular gable stones (Fig. 3). At least eight examples are recorded, including two at Temple Cronan, flanking the east end of the church to north and south (it is easy to miss the northern one which lies behind a wall). At Killabuonia, close together on the upper terrace are a cross-carved pillar, a rectangular slab enclosure, and a tent-shaped slab shrine with a round hole in its west gable stone, presumably to give access to the relics (Fig. 3 and see p. 33). In Ulster are six small house-shaped structures, built of mortared stone and clearly designed to hold burials or relics. At Bovevagh and Tamlaghtard a hand-hole gives access to the interior, and the masonry of the Banagher (Derry) example indicates a twelfth-century date (Fig. 3).

These are some of the traces still visible of the great care lavished on fitting treatment for special burials. The background to enshrining relics and making them accessible to pilgrims lies in Early Christian continental practice, and some elements have continued, as anyone can see from the small, house-shaped structures set up over graves as recently as the eighteenth and nineteenth centuries. Around the focus would cluster the other graves, which leave little trace for us to see except for the carved stones discussed in the next chapter. Excavation shows that some burials were laid in simple graves dug in the earth without stone linings, whilst others were in stone-built cists. These occur widely in western Britain, and like house-shaped monuments are known in some cases to have been built in quite recent times.

Written sources tell us that there were royal graveyards at some important monasteries, at Armagh and Clonmacnois and Reefert church at Glendalough, for instance. But it is difficult to know without large-scale excavation what community a graveyard would be serving, and little excavation of monastic cemeteries has yet been done in Ireland. It is a laborious and difficult task, especially if the area continued in use for burial in medieval and later times, as the excavators of Gallen Priory found in 1935. A monastery provided burial for its *manaig*, and lay people paid burial-fees to churches, but we do not know whether part of the monastic graveyard was set aside for them. Written sources and recent practice testify that special provision has long been made for the burial of exceptional groups. Near the old church at Carrickmore (Tyrone), for example, were graveyards for slain men, who presumably died without the last rites, unbaptized infants and suicides. Women's graveyards are sometimes separate from the main monastic cemetery as on Inishmurray.

These are all the ingredients which combine to make up the plan of early Irish monasteries—enclosure, church and grave-yard, round tower, cells and other buildings. Recent work at Inishcaltra and Reask has shown just how much remains to be discovered by excavation about monastic buildings and planning. At Reask, for example, where five years ago there were only slight traces above ground, the full circuit of the enclosure wall is now clear, with its subdivisions, paths and drains, circular stone hut foundations, a tiny stone oratory and a cemetery of cist graves. The remains which confront the traveller on any particular site are likely to be defective, yet by adding together elements from many sites and calling upon written and excavated evidence he will be able to build up a picture of the material surroundings which formed the background to life in early Irish monasteries (Fig. 5).

5

Stone-carving

Ireland is exceptionally rich in carved stones of the Early Christian period. They often stand close to other remains, but sometimes a splendid cross survives where no other early features can be seen. A rough chronology can be suggested, beginning with pillars and slabs bearing incised crosses, a tradition which continues after the emergence of freestanding crosses with carved decoration in relief. The stone-carving is often beautiful and interesting in itself, but it can also provide a commentary on the church, on its craftsmanship, its foreign contacts, on changing fashions, and even on the appearance of people and buildings. The traveller will inevitably encounter these stones, and questions immediately arise in his mind.

First, what were they for? They served different purposes, as the written sources indicate. They might mark burials, and the most usual formulae in inscriptions ask for a prayer or blessing on a person—OROIT (OR) DO or BENNACHT AR (Fig. 16). Burials were also made at stones already set up: Cuthbert, for example, in seventh-century Northumbria wanted to be buried 'close to the oratory, on the south side, beside the cross I myself set up'. Legislation ordered that the *termon* or holy place, that is the area in which sanctuary could be claimed, should be clearly marked by crosses, and this must be what the ninth-century poem alludes to when it describes 'a pious cloister behind a circle of crosses'. Stories, still current, of seven crosses formerly in the vicinity of particular churches may preserve some tradition of boundary crosses, and when a cross is some distance from a church, as at Kilree, it may have marked a boundary. Crosses may have been used as a focus for outdoor services, and a Rule makes it clear that they were used for penance: 'at the cross, in the presence of the head of the monks . . . with humility, without disputes, let each confess his faults there'. They were also sometimes set up to mark notable events, to commemorate a grant of land, or mark an important place, like the 'cross at the gate of the Rath' at Armagh, and it seems that they were set up along routes, for one of the later Lives of Patrick describes him

Fig. 15   Types of crosses

stopping to pray at every cross he passed on his travels. Cross-carved stones and free-standing crosses were an important element in the topography of early Irish monasteries, and they can be viewed against this wide range of possible functions.

We must look first at those stones which have crosses carved on their face in two dimensions as they are probably earlier in their origins than free-standing, three-dimensional crosses (Figs 17 and 19). The range of crosses varies enormously, from very simple, linear, unembellished forms to quite complicated ringed and expanded crosses and others made of segments of circles (Fig. 15). The cross can be enclosed in a rectangular or circular frame. Sometimes there may be no decoration at all, or the cross can be elaborated, for example with triangular or spiral terminals or an expansion at the crossing, or with decoration of circles, small crosses, interlace, fretwork and occasionally birds or human figures between the arms and shaft. There is great scope for variation on the simple cross theme, and the form can give a clue to the date, though the simpler kinds had a very long life and are rarely closely datable.

The most easily available local material was usually employed, whether this was basalt, slate, limestone, sandstone, granite or some other stone. But fine stone was sometimes transported, especially when this could be done by water: sandstone was taken to Clonmacnois from lower down the Shannon. The amount of preliminary working of the stone varied, from none at all or a little preparation of the face to be carved to careful trimming all over, sometimes to a regular outline. The simplest way of forming a cross was by linear incision with a sharp instrument, but a common method seems to have been pecking, using a hammer and punch, leaving a very distinctive pock-marked surface which was often rubbed and smoothed. An effect of relief could be obtained for parts of the design by working back the general surface of the stone, though it is difficult to see these signs of working if stones are weathered and covered with lichen and moss.

We know very little about who carved these crosses and how far stone-carvers also worked in wood and metal. One stone at Clonmacnois (Fig. 16) brings us close to a particular craftsman, though it is uncertain in what medium he worked. It bears a finely worked, beautifully decorated expansional cross and asks for a prayer for THUATHAL SAER, Tuathal the craftsman. There must have been an important centre of stone-carving at Clonmacnois and others on Inishcaltra and elsewhere, but little is known about exactly how the craft was organized and how ideas and products travelled.

Amongst the earliest cross-carved stones must be those with ogam inscriptions, like the stone at Arraglen, north of Brandon Mountain, which commemorates Ronán the priest, son of Comgán, and the boulder at Maumanorig which reads 'the name of Colmán the pilgrim'. The ogam alphabet, which indicated letters in a rather cumbersome way by groups of lines along the angle of a stone (Fig. 17), was developed in western Britain or Ireland in the late Roman period. There are over three hundred

Fig. 16   Memorial stone of Tuathal the Craftsman at Clonmacnois

ogam inscriptions in Ireland, mostly in Munster, especially in Kerry, Cork and Waterford, the earliest probably belonging to a pre-Christian milieu, but since at least one third occur on sites with some ecclesiastical associations, they were clearly also used in a Christian context. With the spread of Latin scholarship and the far more convenient half-uncial script (seen in Fig. 16), ogam became obsolete, yet a stone from Church Island (off Valencia), on which the ogam is later than a sophisticated cross, suggests its persistence as late as the eighth century. A group of ogam stones

83

is displayed near the Gap of Dunloe (not at a church site), and familiarity with clear examples like these (Fig. 17) will help in recognition of less clear and defaced inscriptions at monastic sites, at Ardfert, Killeen Cormac, Castlekeeran and elsewhere.

Standing stones, a common if rather enigmatic type of prehistoric monument, when carved with crosses, may be among the earliest cross-carved stones in Ireland. They occur either singly or in groups, usually in a prominent position, and occasionally a cross has been added. At Findermore, west of Clogher, for example, is a cross-carved standing stone on a hilltop where Patrick is reported to have preached to a huge congregation, though the cross may well have been cut much later than the fifth century. A cross has been carved on one of the kerb-stones of a Neolithic passage grave at Lough Crew, and on a stone close to another prehistoric burial place, a multiple cist cairn, at Knockane (Fig. 17), perhaps to 'Christianize' places with pagan and malevolent associations (see p. 30). We know this sometimes happened, for the seventh-century Life of the sixth-century British saint Sampson describes how the saint, finding pagans dancing round a stone in Cornwall, converted them and marked a cross on the stone with an iron tool to commemorate the event. This allows us to glimpse one way in which a cross could have been carved on standing stones or other prehistoric monuments.

Upright cross-carved pillar stones (Fig. 17) are common at sites in the islands and coastal counties of western Ireland, but their distribution further east is less dense. They probably range in date through the whole Early Christian period, though some are early, like the stone at Kilmalkedar which is carved with an alphabet as well as a cross, the letters suggesting a sixth-century date (Fig. 17). Features of some stones, especially in the southwest, suggest links with the continent, France and perhaps further east. The *chi-rho* cross, common in continental inscriptions from the fifth century onwards, made up of the first two letters of Christ's name in Greek, *chi* (χ) and *rho* (ρ), of which good examples can be seen in County Kerry at Arraglen, Kilshannig and Knockane (Fig. 17), and the appearance of *alpha* (α) and *omega* (ω) under the arms of the cross, as at Kildrenagh (Loher)

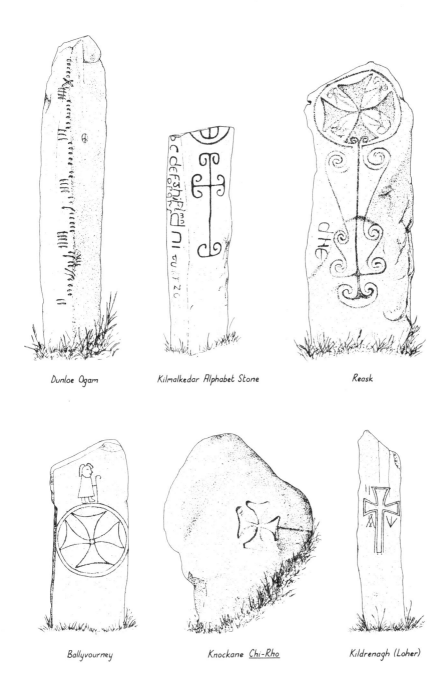

Dunloe Ogam   Kilmalkedar Alphabet Stone   Reask

Ballyvourney   Knockane _Chi-Rho_   Kildrenagh (Loher)

Fig. 17   Inscribed and cross-carved pillars

85

(Fig. 17) are both forms derived from continental models. The beautifully decorated pillar at Reask has the abbreviation *DNE* for the Latin, *Domine*, 'Lord', and must also be early (Fig. 17). These stones, dating probably from the sixth and seventh centuries, show a church not yet confident enough to have developed any highly individual form of cross, probably a church not yet rich enough to exercise patronage over elaborate workmanship. It is a church following continental models in some of its designs, introducing Christian monuments into the Irish countryside and Christian forms of burial to the people.

The earliest pillar closely datable with some confidence by its inscription is the tall stone at Kilnasaggart. It stands in a cemetery of cist graves, and a long inscription commemorates the gift of the place by Ternoc who died, according to annals, in 714 or 716. In this way, by establishing some fixed points by inscriptions and by comparisons with other datable material, manuscripts and metalwork, the outline of a chronological sequence is built up, though many less distinctive stones will not be easy to place within it.

Recumbent stones became the most popular form of gravemarker from the seventh century onwards and persisted until the end of our period in the twelfth. The finest collection is at Clonmacnois, where four to five hundred have been recorded; another rich midland site is Gallen with at least two hundred, and there are other large groups at Inishcaltra and St Berrihert's Kyle, whilst at other sites stones occur in smaller groups or singly. For reasons of safety they have sometimes been re-set, as at Tullylease in a wall cupboard in the church, since flat stones quickly get overgrown, and the smaller ones are all too portable. Indeed the loss rate at Clonmacnois was so serious that all the slabs were built into a display wall to prevent further dispersal, where they form a unique 'teaching collection' of crosses. But it is important to realize that they were originally recumbent over burials, and some can be seen *in situ* in the graveyards at Glendalough, occasionally with a small erect cross or slab at the foot. Inscriptions make it clear that these recumbent slabs were tombstones (Fig. 16), and it is occasionally possible to date them, because many of those commemorated in inscriptions were abbots or other important clerics whose deaths are noted in the monastic annals.

The large Clonmacnois collection illustrates better than any other the range of cross forms and decoration (Fig. 15). Ringed crosses, for example, are very popular on recumbent slabs in the ninth century, whilst expansional crosses, with decorated expansions at the centre and limb ends, date mainly from the tenth to twelfth centuries. These cross-carved stones are less obvious and less well known than the free-standing crosses, but they are rewarding and worth looking for, both at sites like Clonmacnois and Gallen where there are many well-exhibited examples, and also where there are fewer, and some searching out may be needed. The beauty of the cross on the undulating surface of the Reask pillar, the charm of the busily striding figure on the Ballyvourney stone (Fig. 17), the quality of the craftsmanship of some of the Clonmacnois expansional crosses—all these have to be seen and enjoyed.

Best known of the carved stone monuments, and sometimes the most striking feature on the site, are free-standing, three-dimensional crosses, often known as 'high crosses'. The Irish total of large crosses must run into three figures, with parallel series in northern and western Britain, and they are one of the outstanding contributions of the British Isles to Early Christian art, for they are unique to these islands. Within Ireland their distribution is oddly uneven, concentrated in the midlands and the east, with few in the west where other kinds of material remains are usually plentiful. Some of the historically important sites have fine crosses, such as Clonmacnois, Durrow, Kells and Monasterboice, and other great monasteries clearly once had crosses, for battered fragments survive at Armagh, Bangor and Connor, but at some important sites, like Clonard and Lismore, there are none at all. There are also fine crosses at churches which are historically obscure, like Ahenny, Killamery and Killary, and how far the surviving distribution faithfully reflects the original distribution is a difficult question which further research may gradually succeed in clarifying.

The most usual form is a tall ringed cross set in a shapely base, but within this framework there is much scope for variation (Fig. 19). The size ranges from tall examples, eighteen to twenty feet or more in height, as at Arboe, Monasterboice (West Cross) and Moone, to short, stubby crosses, six to eight feet high, as at Duleek. The head is usually (though not always) ringed, the ring sometimes solid but more usually open; the inner circumference of the ring can be decorated with projecting semi-circular discs, though these can also occur in the 'armpits'. When the head is intact, it is usually finished by a finial, sometimes shaped, as we have seen, like a small wooden house or oratory (Fig. 7). The edges of the limbs are finished off with mouldings, which can be quite elaborate, and the face is sometimes subdivided into panels by small mouldings. The most usual shape for the base is a truncated pyramid, though rectangular, cubical and circular bases are also found.

Decoration includes figure carvings, animals and a wide range of geometrical motifs including interlace, spirals, bosses and key patterns. Foliage patterns, like the vine-scrolls so popular in Northumbria, are uncommon, though they are found on the Kells Tower Cross, the South Cross at Clonmacnois and Muiredach's Cross at Monasterboice. The disposition of the scenes, and the relationships of figure to non-figure decoration and to undecorated areas, change with time, and so provide the basis for establishing a chronological sequence. There are other fine crosses with little or no decoration, which rely for their effect on good proportions and carefully worked mouldings, like the three in the graveyard at Castlekeeran near Kells.

The stone which masons preferred for free-standing crosses was sandstone when it was available, and when hard, fine-grained sandstone was used it can survive in wonderfully fresh condition, preserving intricate detail, as it does on Muiredach's Cross, Monasterboice (Figs 4 and 18). But when the stone was softer, as for the West Cross on the same site, or at Arboe, the surface has become badly eroded and much of the detail is lost. When sandstone was not within reach other materials were used: there are groups of granite crosses in County Down and west of the

Wicklow mountains in Counties Kildare and Kilkenny, and limestone crosses in the west. Granite is coarse-textured and very hard, encouraging a flat, simplified style of carving, excluding rounded modelling and careful detailing. The result at Moone,

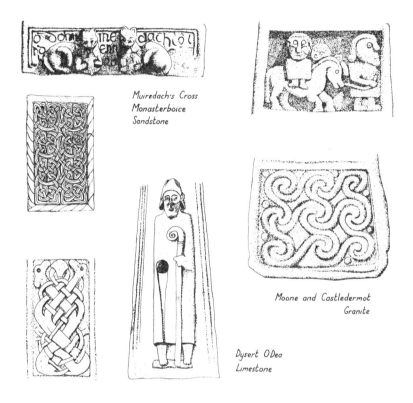

Muiredach's Cross
Monasterboice
Sandstone

Moone and Castledermot
Granite

Dysert ODea
Limestone

Fig. 18   Details of crosses

Castledermot, Ullard and elsewhere is naïve, rather like a cartoon, but most attractive (Fig. 18). In Clare and the Aran Islands crosses were made from the ubiquitous grey slabby limestone, which allows sharply cut detail, both high-relief, like the figures on the Dysert O Dea cross, and intricate low-relief carving (Fig. 18), and these distinctive crosses can also be seen at Kilfenora and at Tighlagh Eany and Temple Brecan on Inishmore.

Crosses were sometimes carved from a single stone, and the problems involved in moving, working and erecting the bigger crosses must have been considerable. In other cases two or more stones were carefully joined by mortice and tenon, and if the cross is incomplete it is sometimes possible to observe the stump of the tenon or the empty mortice hole. A join could be made in the shaft, in which case it was sometimes marked by a decorated 'collar', as at Arboe, or the head could be separately worked, and this may be why it is not uncommon to find an ill-matching head and shaft when fragmentary crosses have been wrongly reconstructed, like the small heads on the larger shafts at Clones and Tuam. Finials and bases were usually separately worked from individual stones. If a cross has been broken and restored it is usually possible to detect the new work: sometimes parts of different crosses are ill matched in size, like the Clones example, or different edge mouldings on the two parts can provide a clue, as at Donaghmore (Tyrone).

A few unfinished crosses remain to show us something of the stages of manufacture. The unfinished cross at Kells (Fig. 19) has large panels blocked out on the shaft and arms, not yet decorated, with the Crucifixion scene partly worked at the crossing and only the ring completed, the delicate interlace contrasting oddly with the unfinished state of the rest. Other unfinished crosses survive, for example at Errigal Keerogue. The reason seems sometimes to have been that a broken limb or a particularly hard vein in the stone discouraged the craftsman from pursuing his work.

The origin of the ringed cross form has been much discussed and there is no very clear answer. The Early Christian cross within a wreath may have influenced its development, or the stone cross may copy an Irish wooden prototype, for in a timber cross the segments of the ring could brace the arms and shafts, and the heads of rivets or pegs holding the wooden joints may be reflected in the projecting stone discs on the ring or in the 'armpits'. We must certainly imagine wooden crosses, perhaps in great numbers and decorated with painting or carving, all now lost, for it is only in exceptional conditions of waterlogging, desiccation or burning that wood survives well. It is also possible that isolated stone cross bases, where no stone shaft is in evidence, once held wooden crosses, as at Castlekeeran.

The dating of crosses, as of churches, is bedevilled by the lack of chronological fixed points, and the notices beside crosses will sometimes offer a bewildering range of some four hundred years to choose from. Some bear inscriptions, and the most famous is the well-preserved one at the base of the shaft of the cross at Monasterboice (Fig. 18), asking for a prayer for Muiredach, unfortunately a very common name, so that, although the inscription is usually linked with an abbot who died in 916, this cannot be regarded as certain. As with churches, the first really firm dates are no earlier than the twelfth century: an unringed cross on Inishcaltra is dated by its inscription to 1111 (or a little before), and at Tuam a cross whose ornament is closely paralleled in the nearby Romanesque cathedral is dated to between 1126 and 1156.

As will be seen, the dating problems undoubtedly exist, but an attempt can be made to outline a widely accepted chronological sequence, with the proviso that it is not universally accepted and that there remains much scope for discussion and argument. Dr Henry has suggested that a group of cross-carved slabs and mono-lithic, slab-like crosses in County Donegal belong to the late seventh century, including the cross at Carndonagh (Fig. 19) and slabs at Drumhallagh and Fahan (Fig. 19). This group of stones is geographically remote and stylistically isolated, and this early date is not uncontested. If, however, these crosses do date from the seventh century they illustrate one way in which Northumbrian influence, evident in the broad ribbon interlaced designs, could have reached Ireland: a mission went from Iona to Northumbria in the seventh century, and Derry, like Iona a foun-dation of Columcille, is close to these sites in the Inishowen peninsula and on Lough Swilly. In the south-west of Ireland, at Tullylease, is a richly decorated slab, with close Anglo-Saxon parallels, commemorating a man with an Anglo-Saxon name, Berichter. He may have been one of those English ecclesiastics who we know were emigrating to Ireland in the late seventh century.

91

Carndonagh

Fahan

Ahenny North

Kells Unfinished

Muiredach's Monasterboice

Fig. 19 Crosses

A series of crosses in western Ossory, studied in detail by Miss Roe, show strong regional characteristics (Ahenny in Fig. 19). They are not tall (eleven to twelve feet high at Ahenny), but have a very large ring and a very long top member, sometimes with an odd, beehive-shaped finial (not certainly original). Angle mouldings are prominent, and there are frequently bosses at the intersection of arms, shaft and ring. Figure and animal decoration is largely confined to their bases, and the shafts are filled with intricate, delicate geometric designs of interlace, spirals and fretwork. There are striking similarities between this decoration and fine eighth-century metalwork, such as the Moylough belt shrine and the Tara brooch (both in the National Museum, Dublin), and an eighth-century date for the group is likely. The main sites are Ahenny, Kilkieran, Killamery and Kilree. These crosses are clearly the work of a confident, well-established church in command of rich patronage, a church which has evolved its own native art styles from the cross which began as a foreign import.

For the Tower Cross at Kells the mason seems to have copied some of his decorative motifs from the Book of Kells, but the date of this manuscript is a matter of controversy. Some scholars have proposed a late eighth- or early ninth-century date for both manuscript and cross. The shaft here shows prominent figure decoration, freely combined with geometric motifs and not confined to framed panels. Rather later, from the ninth and tenth centuries, and perhaps continuing into the eleventh, are the fine crosses on which figure-carving is all-important and is used with a narrative and didactic as well as decorative effect. Most spectacular are the Cross of the Scriptures at Clonmacnois and the crosses at Durrow and Monasterboice, but there are groups in Ulster, many of them badly damaged, and in the area west of the Wicklow granite mountains, as at Castledermot, where figure decoration is combined with spirals reminiscent of prehistoric art (Fig. 18).

There are close parallels between the figure scenes and Carolingian ivories, and analysis of the scenes suggests that some may reflect the content of familiar prayers. There is often a clear Old Testament–New Testament distinction between the two main faces, with the Crucifixion occupying the head on the New

93

Testament side (Fig. 19), and Christ in Glory or a judgement scene in the head on the other side. Old Testament scenes often

Adam and Eve
Arboe

The Ark
Armagh

Sacrifice of Isaac
Arboe

Daniel and Lions
Moone

Jacob and the Angel
Kells Market

The Children in the
Fiery Furnace
Monasterboice West

David the Harpist
Durrow

The Baptism of Christ
Kells Broken Cross

Soldiers at the Tomb
Clonmacnois

Fig. 20   Figure scenes from crosses

illustrate incidents when God has helped those in trouble (Fig. 20)—Noah and the flood, the sacrifice of Isaac, Daniel and the lions, the children in the fiery furnace—and Robin Flower pointed out how these can be seen as a version in stone of prayers based on one in the Roman Breviary, the *commendatio animae*, which appear in several Irish texts of the ninth century. Some of the New Testament scenes illustrate the office of the Epiphany, such as the adoration of the Magi, the annunciation to the shepherds, the feast of Cana and the entry into Jerusalem, and other incidents, including Paul and Antony receiving bread from a raven in the desert (Fig. 7) and the miracle of the loaves and fishes, can be interpreted as having Eucharistic significance. Specially popular were scenes from the heroic David story, particularly David and Goliath, David breaking the lion's jaws, and David the harpist (Fig. 20). Horsemen, chariots and hunting scenes often appear on the bases.

The surviving crosses are often incomplete, mutilated and weathered, and the traveller may have difficulty at first in identifying figure scenes, but from illustrations and from the well-preserved examples he can become familiar with the range of themes and the recurrent grouping of figures, so that, confronted by more fragmentary and weathered crosses, he will be able to recognize many of the more common scenes. There are, however, other figure groups which are much more difficult to interpret and do not seem to be drawn from the Bible. Some may be based on stories which grew up around biblical characters, like the fall of Simon Magus on Kells Market Cross, some may illustrate scenes in a monastery's own history, and some may be derived from the rich store of early Irish myth and legend. These enigmatic scenes certainly provide much scope for speculation.

Close study of the panels of figure-carving shows that certain scenes recur in very similar forms on different crosses, as in the panel showing the soldiers guarding the tomb at Clonmacnois (Fig. 20), Durrow and Kells, or the ark at Armagh, Camus and Kells. There are close similarities, too, between panels of geometric decoration on widely separated crosses. The conclusion seems to be that there were schools or traditions of stone-carving and perhaps pattern-books on which craftsmen could draw. There may have been centres of manufacture, like Armagh and Kells, from which men were sent out to execute commissions elsewhere, but here we are in the realms of speculation, for our evidence does not allow any very firm conclusions.

Irishmen played a quite prominent part in the Carolingian renaissance, and these ninth- and tenth-century crosses, although they are peculiarly Irish in effect, nevertheless show the influence of continental art forms in their figure sculpture and narrative style. Irishmen clearly knew what was happening on the Continent, although they were highly eclectic about which elements they adopted, and transmuted even these into their own idiom.

The latest clearly definable horizon of crosses within our period belongs to the later eleventh and twelfth centuries, and now the emphasis is very different. There are usually a few, often two, very prominent figures in high relief, sometimes with cavities surviving into which separate carved members would be fitted, like the ecclesiastic's hand at Dysert O Dea (Fig. 18). The rest of the surface is sometimes covered with intricate, low-relief decoration, including animal interlace, which has very clear analogies with eleventh- and twelfth-century Viking art styles on metal-work and in manuscripts. The figures can sometimes be recognized as Christ and an ecclesiastic, probably a bishop, for instance at Cashel, Roscrea and Dysert O Dea. The Viking art styles remind us that by the twelfth century the Scandinavian colonizers were playing an important part in the church reform movement. This was a time when the older monasteries, with their dependent, often widely scattered houses, were being superseded by fixed territorial bishoprics (see p. 102), and it is tempting to see these twelfth-century crosses with their prominent bishops as a product of this reforming period. Their distribution is thin in the east and midlands which are rich in earlier crosses, and most concentrated in the west, where the earlier crosses were rare or absent, naturally enough, since the south-western kingdom of Munster played a leading part in the new ecclesiastical movement.

The figure-carved crosses must have served the same purpose as wall-paintings and glass in medieval and modern churches. They can be seen as lessons, prayers in stone, invocations for help, reminders of important events and festivals, and perhaps they conveyed other messages which have become lost over the long span of time separating the crosses from our own day. But one point seems clear: many of the finest crosses must date from the period, broadly 800 to 1000, when the Irish church and much of the countryside was ravaged by Vikings, who were at first pagans. Metal-work did not cease in this period: there has even been a recent attempt to suggest that it was stimulated by the importing of Viking silver. Moreover, the period of severe devastation by the Vikings of the Irish church was comparatively short, from about 830 to the 870s. It may well be, however, that the churches, which the annals prove to have suffered heavily in the ninth-century Viking attacks, were using their resources to patronize craftsmen in stone whose works could not be burned or looted.

As well as these tall, impressive, carefully carved crosses the traveller will encounter many small, often rough crosses, made of local stone, usually undecorated and without any clearly datable features. Their very simplicity presents a problem: some may be old and were perhaps boundary-markers, like the two at Banagher (Derry) where it is alleged there were originally five, but others may have been made to mark graves in quite recent times, and it is not always easy to distinguish early carved stones from much later ones. The difference is clear enough when elaborate workmanship is involved: Muiredach's Cross at Monasterboice is obviously early, whilst the nineteenth-century high crosses marking graves nearby are not, and although graveyards often contain recent copies of early crosses the workmanship and lack of weathering usually leave little room for doubt. But when simple crosses and cross-carved stones have been used as grave-markers, uninscribed and undated, perhaps made with a potentially 'early' technique, like the pecking found in the area of the Mourne Mountains, a practised eye is needed to detect old from new. Familiarity with the general run of stones in a graveyard and in an area will help the observer to pick out what is odd and potentially interesting, but some stones will usually remain in a 'no man's land', not certainly modern and not certainly old.

Although figure-carving is common on the crosses, the Early Christian stone-carvers' repertoire does not seem often to have

97

extended to figure-carving on other kinds of stones, but the examples which do occur are interesting. The two-sided figure in the graveyard on Boa Island and some of the carvings in the north transept of Armagh cathedral must have their roots in a pre-Christian tradition, but the carved figures of ecclesiastics with bells and croziers at Carndonagh, Killadeas and White Island are firmly in a Christian context, and bring us face to face with the artists' view of some Early Christian churchmen.

There are other kinds of carved stones which may be encountered at early church sites. Certain stones with five crosses, seen for example at Clonmacnois (Fig. 15), may be derived from an altar, for legislation shows that, although altars were meant to be of stone, they were often made of wood, and in these cases a stone was to be let into the top, big enough to hold the vessels for the celebration. In medieval times the consecrated stone altar-top, the *mensa*, was marked with five crosses, one in the centre and one at each corner (there is a good fifteenth-century example in Sligo Abbey), and when a stone carved with five crosses in this way occurs at an early monastic site it may be derived from an early altar. Different again are the portable altars, small consecrated blocks of wood or stone, used for services on journeys away from the church, and small, easily portable stones with five crosses may have served this purpose.

The monastic routine revolved around the regular services; rules from the eighth and ninth century when there was an ascetic revival are particularly strict about the observance of canonical hours, and sundials bring us close to this round of services (see p. 5). They are not very common, but good examples can be seen at Bangor, Clogher, Inishcaltra, Kilmalkedar (Fig. 21), Monasterboice and Nendrum. In Anglo-Saxon England sundials are usually found built into the church fabric, as at Kirkdale (Yorks.), and in medieval churches they were often cut on the fabric, for example on a quoin stone. But those early Irish sundials which survive are carefully shaped, free-standing monuments, and we can perhaps imagine them in a position of prominence, close to the church. The most common form is a shaft, sometimes with a semi-circular expanded head, with three rays extending from the gnomon at the top of the semi-circle, presumable indicating terce, sext and none. Further subdivision by intermediate rays is sometimes found, as at Nendrum. Routine can hardly have depended entirely on the sundial, for the sun did not shine all the time in Early Christian Ireland any more than it does today, and we must imagine some member of the commun-

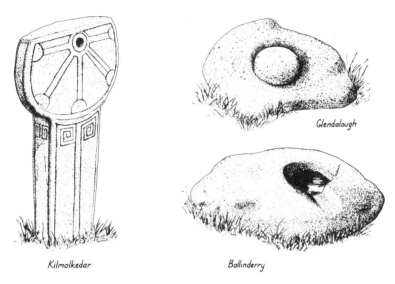

Kilmalkedar   *Ballinderry*   *Glendalough*

Fig. 21   Sundial and bullaun stones

ity responsible for finding and indicating the time, using bells, sundials and whatever other means he had at his disposal.

There is a final class of worked stones which are a common feature of early church sites and have exercised the imagination of many generations of antiquaries: hollowed stones, often called bullauns (Fig. 21). Sometimes there is only one, but at some sites there are several, and at Glendalough over thirty are scattered along the valley. The most common type is a boulder, unworked except for the hollow, either loose and movable or very large, perhaps an earthfast glacial erratic. Though it is difficult to generalize, the diameter of the hollow is often between seven and fifteen inches and the depth between three and nine inches. It is usually roughly circular, though oval examples are not uncommon, the profile varying from gently hemispherical to very steep-sided or even undercut. The stones are often now filled with rainwater, and the water is sometimes used for wart cures.

Many traditions have grown up around bullauns. Single hollows are explained as a saint's pillow and double ones as knee-marks from long prayer vigils, whilst water-filled examples are sometimes called fonts. A few of the stories attached to them have food associations, for a bullaun can be the basin into which a miraculous cow produced her never-failing daily supply of milk, and it is in the homely realm of subsistence that bullauns probably should be viewed. They are ideal for use as mortars, for grinding all kinds of substances with a pestle. The frugal diet described in Columbanus's Rule included vegetables, beans, flour mixed with water, and bread, and crushing and grinding could have been important in the preparation of all these. Rather similar hollowed stones are known to have been used in recent times for crushing apples, pounding furze (whins) for stock, and other domestic purposes, whilst non-food materials, like pigments and metal ores, could have been crushed in stone basins. But even if the original purpose was a homely one it has been oddly lost sight of, and these stones have certainly sometimes been used for other purposes, including curative and superstitious ones. Bullauns are not to be confused with circular, square or polygonal fonts and stoups which are usually carefully shaped, inside and out and are likely to be medieval.

The carved stones of Ireland show us a church developing from rather humble and dependent beginnings into a rich, powerful institution with an elaborate decorative art, drawing inspiration from continental models, from Anglo-Saxon England and Carolingian Gaul, from Viking motifs and from Romanesque patterns, yet all the time transmuting what it learned into its own highly individual style. They provide a feast of visual enjoyment and give us side-lights on the daily life of the monastery, on the appearance of the clerics, and on the craftsmen and their skills, so that through them the informed modern traveller may come face to face with the early Irish church.

6

Present state

By the twelfth century when our main considerations end the Irish church, which had been founded in the fifth century, was adopting the usual administration of the western church, with dioceses and parishes and reformed monastic orders. But since the twelfth century a further eight hundred years have passed, and the vicissitudes of those centuries account for the present appearance of early Irish monastic sites.

When diocesan sees were founded in the twelfth century each diocese had to have its own bishop, and the bishop had a special seat, his *cathedra*. Some of the most important old monasteries were chosen as the sites of cathedral churches, including Clonard, Clonfert, Down, Lismore and others. Sometimes the creation of a see provided an occasion for the building or rebuilding of a church on a suitably grand scale. The elaborately carved west door at Maghera (Derry) could be as late as 1152–73 when the bishop transferred the see there from Ardstraw. At Ardmore there was an attempt to claim episcopal status (though nothing is heard of the diocese after 1210), and Mael Étain Ua Duib Rátha, 'noble priest of Ardmore', died in 1203 'after finishing the building of the church'. A recent study has unravelled the history of the enlarging and adorning of the small early church there whose masonry is still visible in the chancel, setting it in the context of these claims.

Not all cathedral churches on early sites prospered equally. Clonmacnois and Clonard were both declared *cathedra* by the synod of Uisnech (1111), but during the twelfth and thirteenth centuries Clonard, ecclesiastical centre of the powerful Anglo-Norman lordship of Meath, extended her territory at the expense of Clonmacnois, which became one of the poorest Irish sees. In the late fifteenth and early sixteenth centuries Clonmacnois was without an effective resident bishop because of the poverty of the see, and in 1516 eyewitnesses testified before the papal notary that the cathedral was roofless and ruinous. Dublin had become a Viking bishopric subject to Canterbury in the eleventh century, and in 1111 a bishop's *cathedra* had been established at Glendalough, but in 1216 Glendalough was united to Dublin. Estates of the old monastic church of Emly were given to the new archbishopric of Cashel, and Mungret, an obvious place for an episcopal centre, at one time claiming episcopal rank, became the property of the see of Limerick, while Lismore was united to the see of Waterford in 1363. Sees which were economically and politically powerful grew at the expense of more remote and conservative centres.

These examples underline the variety which the traveller can expect to encounter. Some of the cathedrals at early monastic sites are still in use, like Clonfert, Clogher and Downpatrick, but the cathedral churches at Cashel, Clonmacnois and Glendalough are ruined. Some of these cathedrals are large and in thriving towns, like Armagh and Kilkenny, whilst others are small and in much smaller settlements. Cloyne, for example, is a village, and the cathedral at Old Leighlin is in a hamlet, two miles from the larger settlement at Leighlinbridge, a crossing-point over the river Barrow. One of its transepts is ruined and the other has disappeared. In the thirteenth century the bishop of Leighlin proposed that his *cathedra* should be moved to a more convenient site, but tradition was stronger and the cathedral stayed where it was.

In the wake of the new dioceses of the twelfth century came parochial organization, though the parish system was only gradually built up. In the heavily settled Anglo-Irish areas of the east the pattern was one of small, compact parishes, their boundaries often coinciding with the lands of feudal lords, while in the Irish areas parishes seem to have been coterminous with the older population groups. But all over Ireland the old monastic site was often used for the parish church, and so Kells eventually became the centre of a parish, Duleek was for a time a parish church, Roscrea became parochial, and so did very many others. This is why the standing remains at early monastic sites so often turn out to be a parish church. It may be medieval or post-medieval, and it may be intact and still in use or disused and ruined, for the fortunes of churches have varied greatly, and each case needs individual study. Twelfth-century churches are still used for Protestant services at Rahan and Tuamgraney; at Lorrha the ruined nave forms a kind of vestibule to the chancel, still in use; at Lynally the decay is far advanced, and a nineteenth-century church replacing the old one some distance away is itself in a bad state; at many sites there now stands a disused and rapidly decaying eighteenth- or nineteenth-century Protestant church, as at the important early monasteries of Durrow and Terryglass.

Although the Republic of Ireland is a Catholic country it is usually the Protestant church—cathedral or parish church—which occupies the early site. This is not only the case in the north, at Armagh, for instance, where the Protestant cathedral crowns the hilltop which the ancient monastic enclosure once surrounded. In the south, at Kilkenny, Killaloe, Tuam and very many other places the same pattern is evident. This is because in the sixteenth century, when the English kingdom accepted the Reformation, the churches were declared independent of Rome, and the Protestant Church of Ireland is heir to the church of Henry VIII and Elizabeth.

Catholic churches are nearly all fairly modern and they rarely occupy early monastic sites, but they do follow the old tradition in that they are in accessible places and at centres of population where they can best minister to the people. There was, however, one unhappy time when some early monastic sites were put to a very special use by Catholics. During the period of penal legislation, especially from 1691 onwards, the practice of religion by Catholics was severely restricted. Mass was said in private houses, and in the country shelters were sometimes built for services, or a conveniently flat stone in a secluded place was used as an altar. Sometimes an early monastic site provided a suitable place for worship and the 'mass-rock' which served as an altar may be preserved. When penal legislation was relaxed, the new Catholic church in a few cases was built on the site which had gained strong associations during the bad period, so that

104

there are examples of Catholic churches at early monastic sites, and this goes against the general trend already outlined. One example is Tamlaghtard, where the Catholic church stands beside the ancient graveyard and a still-frequented holy well.

In England there are many thousands of medieval parish churches still in use, but in Ireland only a handful. Whereas in England churches have been constantly enlarged, restored and embellished or rebuilt on the same spot, in Ireland a new church has often been built near the old one, perhaps because land was more readily available and less valuable than in strongly nucleated English villages. Thus a common sight in Ireland is a ruined church in the graveyard of a church still in use (and a ruined house close to an inhabited one).

There are many periods and circumstances in which decay may have set in. Some of the more remote early churches were not suitable for parochial centres, and their decay may have begun in the twelfth century, if not earlier. Such churches are today easier to reconstruct in the imagination as early Irish monasteries than those which have had extensive medieval and modern rebuilding. When the Anglo-Norman area of settlement shrank in the fourteenth and fifteenth centuries, settlements must have been deserted and churches abandoned. In the sixteenth and seventeenth centuries, especially in the areas of plantation of settlers, there were concentrations of population at new centres, and the old church was sometimes abandoned for one at a more convenient place. To provide the resources to build a new church, or elaborate an old one, was one of the ambitions of the rich all through the middle ages and well into the modern period—a mark of devotion and a religious duty—but also a status symbol, and so we find new churches being built right down to the nineteenth century. At Ballinderry (Antrim) there are three parish church sites: the earliest, possibly an early monastery and the first parish church, is beside Portmore Lough; the second, the middle church, is a seventeenth-century building a mile to the east, and the move to the present Church of Ireland church two miles further east took place in 1834. But when the Church of Ireland was disestablished in 1869, some churches in areas where support was weak were abandoned, and subsequently a prosperous congregation has been necessary for survival. Where this is lacking, churches have often decayed.

The remains at some sites important in the Early Christian period belong not to the early monastery but to a medieval monastic occupation. Before the twelfth century the indigenous forms of monasticism were current everywhere in Ireland, but in the twelfth century continental orders were being introduced. The Benedictines were never popular in Ireland, though they did settle at Down and Nendrum, but the Cistercians, who followed a reformed version of the Benedictine Rule, leading a communal life of prayer and work, were welcomed, for their asceticism suited the Irish monastic ideal. Usually the Cistercians settled on a completely new site, for they wanted solitude for the community, and a Cistercian house like Mellifont, with its communal buildings around a cloister, forms an instructive contrast to an old-style monastery like Monasterboice, three miles to the northeast. The Augustinian Canons were also popular, and though leading a celibate life under religious rule they wanted to be near people to whom they might minister; so they often set up their establishments in the old monastic centres, usually building new churches, as at Armagh, Bangor, Devenish, Ferns, Glendalough and elsewhere, whilst Augustinian nuns were settled at early sites including Clonmacnois and Killevy. The Romanesque church at Monaincha, which must have replaced an earlier church, was probably built for Augustinian Canons in the second half of the twelfth century, and St Michael, Ballinskelligs, to which the monks from Skellig Michael had already moved, became a house of Augustinian Canons, perhaps early in the thirteenth century. In all about half of the 120 or so Irish Augustinian houses were at or near early monasteries, and where monastic life had continued to the twelfth century the Augustinian Rule was sometimes adopted by the existing community.

Monastic churches suffered the same fate in Ireland as in England when the monasteries were dissolved in the sixteenth century, for they were made over to private owners, who might not maintain them and might even use them as a source of building material. So Mayo, founded for English exiles in the seventh century, made a *cathedra* in the twelfth and united to the see of Tuam in the thirteenth, became the centre of an abbey of Augustinian Canons in the fourteenth, and was granted to a layman, John Rawson, in 1594. All that remains are fragments of buildings and traces of the enclosure. In 1538 the Augustinian house at Ferns was rented to Thomas Alen, and the property then included church and belfry, dormitory, chapter-house, hall and other buildings. By 1600 almost all the monasteries had been secularized, and now traces of an Augustinian abbey or priory, less commonly a house of some other order, are often to be seen at an early site.

Catholics today feel a strong identity with their early saints. Even when an ancient graveyard now surrounds a Protestant church it may be used by Catholic families for burial, and many graveyards round deserted and ruined churches on early sites are still in use. The more venerated the place, the denser will the burials be (Fig. 22): even if the lawns around Armagh cathedral are partly clear of stones, the graves are there, spanning perhaps 1500 years. The strong desire of Christians at all periods to be buried near a specially venerated focus has led in Ireland, as elsewhere, to the intensive use of ancient graveyards, inside as well as outside churches. Thus many early sites are partly sealed to the archaeologist and structures are probably damaged by the long-continued burial, but burial is one of their primary functions now as in the past (see p. 33).

The present appearance of an early monastic cemetery will depend very much on its later history. If it has been used recently for burial the modern gravestones will be prominent, but if burial ceased long ago there may be simply rough, uninscribed stones. Some early sites, especially those long disused and rather remote, have been used for the burial of unbaptized infants. These graveyards are known by several names, including *cillín*, *ceallú-rach* and *cealltrach*, and the graves may be marked by small mounds and rough unlettered stones.

Most ancient graveyards have become raised above their general surroundings, and it is surprising to see how deeply buried some churches have become, like St Declan's 'House' at Ardmore or Dulane church, buried almost to the lintel of its west door. Constant disturbance of the soil over many generations and the long accumulation of organic matter help to produce these distinctive mounds. Sometimes, however, a natural hillock was chosen for a graveyard, like the glacial mound at Killeen Cormac, and excavation at Kilnasaggart showed that the graveyard area had been artificially heightened to create a greater depth for burials.

Early sites are often a focus for pilgrims. On the saint's festival big crowds gather at important sites and the graveyard is tidied beforehand: even the slabs are sometimes scrubbed. Glencolumbkille is full of pilgrims on 9 June making the rounds, visiting special 'stations' on a fixed route to pray at each one. These stations may be parts of buildings, crosses or slabs, cairns, boulders, wells or other features connected with the saint. At Glencolumbkille there are fifteen stations on a three-mile route, and the full round takes about three and a half hours. St Ciarán's day on 9 September is similarly observed at Clonmacnois. The recent excavations on Inishcaltra have uncovered paths which were used on medieval pilgrimage rounds, and the small offerings left at many early sites show that they are still centres of devotion. But pilgrimage features can puzzle the archaeologist. Are the altar-like structures, known as *leachta*, at Inishmurray and other western coastal sites features of the early monastic occupation, or are they comparatively recent pilgrimage foci? Some simple incised crosses at much-frequented sites, like Ballyvourney, Killabuonia and Tullylease, have certainly been made by recent visitors scraping a stone with a pebble during rounds.

Rounds often include a well, and there must be several thousand holy wells in Ireland, many of them at early church sites. There were pressing practical reasons for building a church close to a good water supply, and it is surely this source which has sometimes come to be regarded as a holy well. The well is most commonly a spring, but sometimes a hollowed stone which collects water, like an empty cross socket or a mortar, is now regarded as a holy well. Some springs are abandoned and forgotten, but some are remembered and still visited for cures. If a cup is provided or if coins or other gifts are in the water then the well is still frequented. Sometimes bandages are tied to a nearby tree or crutches have been left as a proof of healing, as they have been at Doon Well (Donegal) and Faughart. In the summer of 1975 a crutch with other gifts was to be seen on St Gobnet's grave, which is a cairn in Ballyvourney graveyard, and we may recall that a tenth-century English poet, describing St Swithun's tomb at Winchester, referred to crutches and cripples' stools around the shrine, left by grateful pilgrims. There are also stories of curses made by turning stones in graveyards, and some stones look as if they have been used for the homely purpose of grinding knife blades. But whatever the reason—praying, curing, blessing, cursing, grinding—all these are signs that early ecclesiastical sites continue to be frequented.

Although some sites, like Clonmacnois, Glendalough and Kells, are rich in early remains, the fragmentary nature of the material at others will strike any visitor forcibly. What were the causes of this damage and destruction? The dissolution of the monasteries has already been mentioned, and a number of monasteries were already in a delapidated state before the dissolution owing to exploitation by superiors and lay lords. Churches have also suffered no less than secular buildings in natural and man-made disasters. The annals tell of lightning causing accidental fires, to which timber buildings would be especially vulnerable; churches have been damaged in warfare, for example the late twelfth-century Anglo-Norman invasion and Edward Bruce's early fourteenth-century campaigns, as well as during bitter conflicts in the sixteenth, seventeenth and late eighteenth centuries. The cathedral at Armagh was turned into a military garrison and fortified with a rampart in the 1560s, and a pictorial map of the town drawn in about 1600 shows six or seven roofless churches; only the cathedral was still partly roofed, and most other buildings were shown as piles of rubble. A church at Derry was used as a powder magazine and badly damaged by an explosion in 1568, whilst the top of Roscrea round tower was demolished in 1789 because it had been used by snipers. Churches may also have

Fig. 22 Clonmacnois from the east

been damaged by their use as store-houses for grain and refuges for fugitives.

Crosses have suffered, especially in the north, during sectarian quarrels, and the fragmentary state of several, including the one in Armagh cathedral, is the result of maltreatment during such conflict. Parts of crosses have been rescued from use as gateposts, water-troughs and the bases of town stocks, and sockets and other cuts which are obviously secondary to the decoration may result from such ill-treatment. Worked stones have been found built into later churches or graveyard walls, and there is still much scope for finding interesting stones in walls as well as loose in graveyards. Several of the fine carved figures on White Island were found re-used in the Romanesque church, whilst the inscribed cross-carved stone also preserved on the site was built into the wall round the church in the nineteenth century and only quite recently rediscovered.

Veneration for early churches has not protected some sites from levelling for agriculture or interference by roads and railways. The round towers at Cloyne, Clondalkin and Roscrea are separated from the nearby churches by roads, and a road was

driven right through the graveyard at Ardstraw. Urban development has been particularly voracious: at Armagh there are now
remains of only two medieval churches, whilst from written
evidence we know of at least eight pre-Norman churches.
Recently, some fine twelfth-century architectural fragments were
found built into an eighteenth-century wall, not far from the site
of the Augustinian church of SS. Peter and Paul, consecrated in
1126. All this destruction, casual and deliberate, means that much
has been lost, but discoveries are still being made.

These sites will be found in very varying physical condition.
Many are overgrown with brambles, ivy, nettles and thorn
bushes, the kind of wilderness from which Bishop Reeves in 1844
disentangled the remains of the important lost site of Nendrum,
where the 'old lime-kiln' was the base of the round tower. Winter
or early spring are the best times for the overgrown sites. At the
other end of the spectrum are the best-kept of the early church
sites in state care, about 150 in the Republic and 22 in Northern
Ireland, and here there will sometimes be signs of restoration and
rebuilding. The modern practice is to make clear the distinction
between original work and restoration by contrasting stone, by

111

inserting a damp-course, or in some other way, but earlier restorers often did not take such care. Inishmurray and Nendrum are examples of sites where there was extensive and poorly recorded restoration which cannot easily be distinguished from original work. Parts of crosses have sometimes been restored in stone or concrete in recent times, and then the contrast between old and new work should be clear from the materials and workmanship. A few buildings or parts of buildings have actually been moved, for re-use or to save them from destruction: the twelfth-century door at Kilmore cathedral (Cavan) is from a church on Trinity Island, Lough Oughter, three miles away, whilst St Molua's stone-roofed church was moved to Killaloe in 1929 from Friar's Island higher up the Shannon because of a hydro-electric scheme.

Some churches have suffered yet more bizarre fates, and each traveller will doubtless make his own collection of oddities. At least two churches on early sites have been made into handball alleys: at Ullard the alley abuts the east end, but at Grangefertagh it occupies the nave and chancel, whilst the east window and west door are to be found re-used in a church several miles away. Some churches have been used as houses, and the larger church at Liathmore shows alterations for domestic use. The prominent steeple on Church Island, Lough Beg (Derry), was added to the ruined church on the early monastic site in 1788 by the earl of Bristol, Bishop of Derry, to improve the view from Ballyscullion House over a mile away.

What has become of the relics and treasures which once adorned these churches? The books, shrines, bells, croziers, and other objects have most commonly been destroyed and dispersed. Many were seized by government order at the time of the Reformation in the 1530s, including Patrick's crozier, the Staff of Jesus, one of the most precious of all relics, burned at Dublin in 1538. These precious things were often in the care of a family of 'keepers', a hereditary office which sometimes persisted to the last century, but gradually material passed to collectors, museums and libraries. And so the Stowe Missal from Lorrha is in the Royal Irish Academy, Dublin, and the books of Armagh, Durrow and

Kells are in Trinity College Library. The shrine of St Laichtín's arm is no longer at Freshford but in the National Museum in Dublin, and St Ruadán's bell from Lorrha is in the British Museum in London. But sometimes objects have stayed in the neighbourhood of the sites and can be seen. It is well worth making the short journey from Lemanaghan to Boher Catholic church at Grogan to see the magnificent twelfth-century shrine of St Manchán. The bell at Fenagh is kept in the parish priest's house, whilst St Bronach's bell from Kilbroney is in the Catholic church at Rostrevor nearby.

The traveller who looks at early Irish monastic sites can see 1500 years of Ireland's varied tradition—rich and proud early settlements, small ascetic sites, medieval parish churches and reformed medieval monasteries, churches of the Protestant ascendancy, and the graveyards where modern Catholics seek burial beside their saints. The sites, as we see them now, mirror the changing kaleidoscope of Ireland's past. The holiday-maker may choose to linger in the western areas of Ireland, exploring the splendid coastline of the Waterville and Dingle peninsulas, the dazzling limestone of Clare and Aran, the islands of Mayo and Sligo and the mountains and inlets of Donegal. Although these areas are not altogether typical of the Irish church, with the exception of the great midland and eastern sites like Clonmacnois, Glendalough, Kells and Monasterboice, they probably give the clearest impression of what an early monastery was like, for it is easier imaginatively to repeople a deserted early ruin like Killabuonia than a modern parish church in urban surroundings like Tallaght in the suburbs of Dublin. It is probably in these western sites that the modern traveller comes nearest to the heart of early Irish monasticism.

Suggestions for further reading

Lord Killanin and M. V. Duignan, *The Shell Guide to Ireland* (2nd edition London, 1969) is an excellent detailed guide, with a glossary of the Irish words which frequently occur in place names included in its excellent apparatus, but it is heavy to carry. P. Harbison, *Guide to the National Monuments of Ireland* (revised edition Dublin 1975, in paperback), which deals only with the Republic, has useful notes on access, a bibliography after each site and a glossary. For Northern Ireland there are two paperback volumes published by H.M.S.O.—*Ancient Monuments of Northern Ireland*, I. In State Care (Belfast 1966), II. Not in State Care (Belfast 1969). *The A.A. Illustrated Road Book of Ireland* (Dublin 1966) has useful maps. *The Ordnance Survey Map of Monastic Ireland* (Dublin 1964) gives many sites important in the Early Christian period whether or not anything remains to be seen. E. R. Norman and J. K. S. St Joseph, *The Early Development of Irish Society: the Evidence of Aerial Photography* (Cambridge 1969) reveals sites in a way impossible from ground-level.

The best general book for the newcomer to Ireland which we know is L. Bieler, *Ireland, Harbinger of the Middle Ages* (London, New York, Toronto 1966). If you want to know about the sources used in the present book, go to Kathleen Hughes, *Early Christian Ireland: Introduction to the Sources* (London 1972: in paperback). She has also written a history of *The Church in Early Irish Society* (London 1966). Françoise Henry has three volumes on early Irish art, each with about 100 superb plates: *Irish Art ... to 800* (London 1965), *Irish Art during the Viking Invasions* (London 1967), *Irish Art during the Romanesque Period* (London 1970; the last two volumes also in paperback). H. G. Leask, *Irish Churches and Monastic Buildings* Vol. I (Dundalk 1955), has not yet been superseded. 114

On more detailed aspects of the subject see F. Henry, *Irish High Crosses* (Dublin 1964, paperback); H. Roe, *The High Crosses of Kells* (1959, paperback) and *The High Crosses of Western Ossory* (1958, paperback); Colm Ó Lochlainn, 'Roadways in Ancient Ireland', *Féil-sgríbhinn Eóin mhic Néill* ed. J. Ryan (Dublin 1940), pp. 465–74; P. Ó Riain, 'Boundary Association in Early Irish Society', *Studia Celtica* VII (1972) 12–29; A. T. Lucas, 'Cloth Finishing in Ireland', *Folk Life Journal* VI (1968) 18–67; 'Washing and Bathing in Ancient Ireland', *Journal of the Royal Society of Antiquaries of Ireland* XCV (1965) 65–114; 'The Sacred Trees of Ireland', *Journal of the Cork Historical and Archaeological Society* LXVIII (1963) 16–54; H. F. McClintock, *Old Irish and Highland Dress* (Dundalk, 1950). There is an excellent relevant bibliography in Chapter 2 of D. Ó Corráin, *Ireland before the Normans* (Dublin and London 1972, paperback).

Further suggestions for reading (1977-97)

It is only possible to point to some of the many publications from the years since 1977, but there are groups of valuable papers in several journals. These include *Peritia* (from 1982 onwards), the *Journal of the Royal Society of Antiquaries of Ireland (J.R.S.A.I.)*, the *Proceedings of the Royal Irish Academy (P.R.I.A.)* and the *Ulster Journal of Archaeology (U.J.A.)*.

Peter Harbison has published a new *Guide to the National and Historic Monuments of Ireland* (Dublin, 1992), covering all of Ireland, and *Historic Monuments of Northern Ireland* (H.M.S.O., Belfast, 1987) deals with the north. Archaeological surveys of several counties or regions have appeared, including *County Donegal* (Lifford, 1983), the *Dingle Peninsula* (Ballyferriter, 1986), *County Louth* (Dublin, 1991), *West Cork* (Dublin, 1992) and the series is continuing.

Two important papers on the organisation and development of the early Irish church are by Donnchadh Ó Corráin, 'The Early Irish Church: Some Aspects of Organisation', in *Irish Antiquity*, ed. D. Ó Corráin (Cork, 1981; reprinted Dublin 1994), 327-41, and Richard Sharpe, 'Some Problems Concerning the Organisation of the Church in Early Medieval Ireland', in *Peritia* 3 (1984), 230-70.

Recently Colmán Etchingham has thrown new light on the organisation of the church in 'The Implications of *Paruchiae*', in *Ériu* 44 (1993), 139-62 and 'Bishops in the Early Irish Church: a Reassessment', in *Studia Hibernica* 1995. Dáibhí Ó Cróinín's *Early Medieval Ireland 400-1200* (London, 1995) includes interesting reflections on the conversion period, and Richard Sharpe discusses 'Churches and Communities in Early Medieval Ireland: Towards a Pastoral Model', in *Pastoral Care Before the Parish*, eds John Blair and Richard Sharpe (Leicester, 1992), 81-109.

Liam de Paor brings together and discusses a wide range of sources relating to Patrick in *Saint Patrick's World: The Christian Culture of Ireland's Apostolic Age* (Dublin, 1993). Máire Herbert looks at the Columban churches in *Iona, Kells and Derry: the History and Hagiography of the Monastic* Familia *of Columba* (Oxford, 1988; reprinted Dublin 1996). Lisa M. Bitel's *Isle of the Saints: Monastic Settlement and Christian Community in Early Ireland* (Cork, 1993) draws on the rich store of saints' Lives. In *J.R.S.A.I* 114 (1984), 5-23 Lisa Bitel considers a subject which interested Kathleen Hughes (see pp 7-9) in 'Women's Donations to the Churches in Early Ireland'.

The Archaeology of Early Medieval Ireland by Nancy Edwards (London, 1990) is a very useful survey with a full reading list, and Michael Ryan's *Irish Archaeology Illustrated* (paperback, Dublin, 1994) provides a well-illustrated introduction to the early medieval period (part v). For an illuminating discussion of ecclesiastical place-names (p. 29) see Deirdre Flanagan, 'The Christian Impact on Early Ireland: the Place-Names Evidence', in *Ireland and Europe: the Early Church*, eds Próinséas Ní Chatháin and Michael Richter (Stuttgart, 1984), 25-51.

Leo Swann has made a special study of ecclesiastical enclosures (pp 54-7) from the air: 'Enclosed Ecclesiastical Sites and their Relevance to Settlement Patterns of the First Millennium A.D.', in *Landscape Archaeology in Ireland*, eds T. Reeves-Smyth and F. Hamond (Oxford, 1983), 269-94, and see also Vincent Hurley, 'The Early Church in the South-West of Ireland: Settlement and Organisation', in *The Early Church in Western Britain and Ireland*, ed. Susan M. Pearce (Oxford, 1982), 297-332.

Several papers on early churches (pp 57-69) have been published, including C.A.R. Radford, 'The Earliest Irish Churches', in *U.J.A.* 40 (1977), 1-11, Peter Harbison, 'Early Irish Churches', in *Die Iren und Europa im früheren Mittelalter*, ed. H. Löwe (Stuttgart, 1982), 618-29, and Ann Hamlin, 'The Study of Early Irish Churches', in *Ireland and Europe: the Early Church* (as above), 117-26. Michael Hare and Ann Hamlin, 'The Study of Early Church Architecture in Ireland: an Anglo-Saxon Viewpoint', in *The Anglo-Saxon Church*, eds L.A.S. Butler and R.K. Morris (London, 1986), 131-45 deals

117

with churches and round towers. For details of individual round towers (pp 69-73) see George Lennox Barrow, *The Round Towers of Ireland* (Dublin, 1979), but his early dating is not acceptable. Ann Hamlin, 'The Archaeology of the Irish Church in the Eighth Century', in *Peritia* 4 (1985), 279-99 focuses on the range of features at ecclesiastical sites in the eighth century. Richard Warner emphasises the defensive function of souterrains (pp 76-7) in 'The Irish Souterrains and their Background', in *Subterranean Britain*, ed. H. Crawford (London, 1979), 100-44. The work at Reask (p. 79) was published by T. Fanning, 'Excavation of an Early Christian Cemetery and Settlement at Reask, County Kerry', *in P.R.I.A.* 81 C (1981), 67-172.

A great deal has been published on stone-carving since 1977. Recent county inventories have already been mentioned, and J.G. Higgins has produced a detailed regional study: *The Early Christian Cross Slabs, Pillar Stones and Related Monuments of County Galway* (Oxford, 1987). On the possible functions of crosses (pp 80-1) see Ann Hamlin, 'Crosses in Early Ireland: the Evidence from Written Sources', in *Ireland and Insular Art A.D. 500-1200*, ed. Michael Ryan (Dublin, 1987), 138-40. On craftsmen (p. 82) see Douglas MacLean, 'The Status of the Sculptor in Old-Irish Law and the Evidence of the Crosses', in *Peritia* 9 (1995), 125-55, and for ogam-inscribed stones (pp 83-4) see Damian McManus, *A Guide to Ogam* (Maynooth, 1991). Michael Herity writes about 'The Chi-Rho and Other Early Cross Forms', in *Aquitaine and Ireland in the Middle Ages*, ed. Jean Michel Picard (Dublin, 1995), 232-60 (pp 84-6). Cathy Swift urges caution in dating cross-carved stones (pp 86-7) in 'Dating Irish Grave Slabs: the Evidence of the Annals', in *From the Isles of the North. Early Medieval Art in Ireland and Britain*, ed. Cormac Bourke (Belfast, 1995), 245-9.

The most important publication since 1977 on free-standing crosses (pp 87-97) is Peter Harbison's *The High Crosses of Ireland: an Iconographical and Photographic Survey* (3 vols., Bonn, 1992). Hilary Richardson and John Scarry have published *An Introduction to Irish High Crosses* (Cork, 1990). In 'Irish High Crosses: Some Evidence from the Plainer Examples', in *J.R.S.A.I.* 116 (1986), 51-67, Dorothy Kelly suggests a total of 'just over three hundred crosses or fragments of crosses' which points to about 270 individual examples (p. 87). The same author's 'The Heart of the Matter: Models for Irish High Crosses', in *J.R.S.A.I.* 121 (1991), 105-45, looks in detail at the structural features of crosses (p. 88). An important contribution to the question of dating crosses (p. 91) is Liam de Paor's 'The High Crosses of *Tech Theille* (Tihilly), Kinnitty, and Related Sculpture', in *Figures from the Past. Studies on Figurative Art in Christian Ireland,* ed. Etienne Rynne (Dun Laoghaire, 1987), 131-58. Roger Stalley considers crosses in a European context in 'European Art and the Irish High Crosses', in *P.R.I.A.* I.O.C (1990), 135-58. See also his booklet on *Irish High Crosses* in the Eason 'Irish History Series' (Dublin, 1991). For the Donegal group of crosses and slabs (p. 91) see Peter Harbison, 'A Group of Early Christian Carved Stone Monuments in County Donegal', in *Early Medieval Sculpture in Britain and Ireland,* ed. John Higgett (Oxford, 1986), 49-71, and Nancy Edwards discusses the Ossory group (p. 93) in 'An Early Group of Crosses from the Kingdom of Ossory', in *J.R.S.A.I.* 113 (1983), 5-46. Ann Hamlin looks at sundials (pp 98-9) in 'Some Northern Sundials and Time-Keeping in the Early Irish Church', in *Figures from the Past* (as above), 29-42. *'The Work of Angels': Masterpieces of Celtic Metalwork, 6th to 9th centuries AD,* ed. Susan Youngs (London, 1989) is a fine survey of metalwork, much of it ecclesiastical, and includes a full bibliography.

List of recommended sites

You will need a good large-scale map, and though some church sites are well kept others are very neglected, so be prepared for nettles. Islands are often only accessible in good weather. The first reference in brackets is to the grid square on the map (between pages 6–7), on which the listed sites are underlined. The four-figure co-ordinates which follow refer to the Ordnance Survey half-inch series and they can also be used with the Northern Ireland one-inch map series.

CO. ANTRIM

ANTRIM (K3; O.S.5, J 15 88) One of two intact round towers in the north. Access across railway, N. of town.

CO. ARMAGH

ARMAGH (J4; O.S.8, H 88 45) Medieval hilltop cathedral, much restored in C19. Cross fragments, carved stones in N. transept and interesting street plan.

KILLEVY (J5; O.S.9, J 04 22) Early church to W., joined to later church to E. Cross-carved stone.

KILNASAGGART (K5; O.S.9, J 06 15) Inscribed pillar-stone in cemetery (graves not visible), with small cross-carved stones. Access past farm, across fields.

TYNAN (J4; O.S.8, H 77 43) Cross in village (made up of two); fragments in graveyard and built into wall; three crosses in Tynan Abbey demesne (private).

CO. CAVAN

KILMORE (G6; O.S.8, H 38 04) Romanesque door from Trinity Island built into cathedral.

CO. CLARE

DYSERT O DEA (D9; O.S.14, R 28 85)   Romanesque church and round tower; C12 cross in field to E.

KILFENORA (D9; O.S.14, R 18 94)   Ruined late Romanesque cathedral and four crosses, one outside churchyard in field to W.

KILLALOE (E10; O.S.18, R 70 73)   St Flannan's stone-roofed church beside cathedral; Romanesque door, cross, finial and stone with ogam and runes inside cathedral; St Molua's church from Friar's Island beside R.C. church up the hill.

OUGHTMAMA (D9; O.S.14, M 31 08)   Three churches in dramatic limestone Burren landscape: fairly rough walk.

SCATTERY ISLAND (C10; O.S.17, Q 97 52)   Churches and round tower, by boat from Cappa Pier.

TEMPLE CRONAN, Termon (D9; O.S.14, M 29 00)   Two slab-shrines N. and S. of church. Access by unsurfaced road, past farm.

CO. CORK

BALLYVOURNEY (D13; O.S.21, W 20 77)   Cross-carved pillar N.E. of village; St Gobnet's 'house', well, and grave near C. of I. church S.W. of village.

KILNARUANE (C14; O.S.24, V 98 48)   Carved pillar-stone, S.W. of Bantry.

TULLYLEASE (D11; O.S.21, R 36 19)   Church and good collection of slabs including one to Berichter.

CO. DERRY

BANAGHER (H2; O.S.4, C 67 07)   Nave with fine W. door, probably early C12; chancel added about 1200, with monumental tomb of same period to S.E. Two small crosses and bullaun. Other tombs at BOVEVAGH (H2; O.S.4, C 66 14) and TAMLAGHTARD (H2; O.S.2, C 68 31).

DUNGIVEN (H2; O.S.4, C 69 08)   Church with C12 nave and C13 chancel.

MAGHERA (J3; O.S.4, C 85 00)   Much-altered early church with elaborate C12 carved lintel in shadow of added tower. Cross-carved stone to W. Notice at graveyard gate about keys.

CO. DONEGAL

CARNDONAGH (H1; O.S.1, C 46 45) Cross may be C7, with two carved flanking stones beside road, W. of village; in graveyard carved pillar and lintel.

CARROWMORE (H1; O.S.2, C 51 45)   Two crosses (in two fields), bullaun and pillar-stone.

DRUMHALLAGH (G2; O.S.1, C 29 32)   Decorated cross-slab N. of Rathmullan.

FAHAN (G2; O.S.1, C 34 26)   Decorated cross-slab, probably C7, in graveyard; cross-carved stone built into graveyard wall.

GLENCOLUMBKILLE (E3; O.S.3, G 53 85)   Fifteen 'stations' cover a large area, many with cross-carved pillars; some easily seen near C. of I. church, but others to N. need more searching out.

CO. DOWN

DERRY, Ards (L4; O.S.9, J 61 52)   Two small churches, S. with *antae*, N., later, without.

MAGHERA (K5; O.S.9, J 37 34)   Round tower stump, surprisingly far N.W. of oval graveyard with C13 church ruin and cross-carved stones.

NENDRUM (L4; O.S.5, J 52 64)   Enclosures, church, cells, round tower, cross-slabs; excavated site on island in Strangford Lough, accessible by road.

ST JOHN'S POINT (L5; O.S.9, J 53 34)   Early church with *antae*; well and bullaun to E.

CO. FERMANAGH

DEVENISH (G4; O.S.8, H 22 47)   C12 round tower (can be climbed) and excavated base of another nearby; C12 St

Molaise's 'House', *Teampull Mór* of about 1200 and later Abbey; many loose carved stones. Island site in Lower Lough Erne, accessible by boat from Enniskillen or from boathouse on lough shore to N.E. (signposted).

INISHMACSAINT (G4; O.S.7, H 16 54) Enclosure surrounds altered early church and large plain cross. Island site in Lower Lough Erne.

KILLADEAS (G4; O.S.7, H 20 54) Figure-carved stone, cross-slab and other stones in C. of I. graveyard.

WHITE ISLAND (G4; O.S.3, H 17 60) Romanesque church, with earlier carved figures set against N. wall, and inscribed slab to W. Island in Lower Lough Erne; boat from shore at Castle Archdale.

CO. GALWAY

ANNAGHDOWN (D8; O.S.14, M 29 38) Cathedral and priory with good Romanesque work.

ARAN ISLANDS (O.S.14) INISHMORE In Killeany townland (C9; L 88 07): Temple Benen, tiny church, orientated N.-S., on limestone height and Tighlagh Eany (St Enda's church) with *antae*, near shore. In Kilmurvy townland: Temple MacDuagh (B9; L 82 10) church with *antae* and added chancel and Temple Brecan (B8; L 81 12) much-altered church, cross fragments and slabs. INISHMAAN (C9; L 94 04) Kilcanonagh church. INISHEER (C9; L 98 02) Kilgobnet church.

CLONFERT (F8; O.S.15, M 96 21) Cathedral has the most elaborate of all Irish Romanesque W. fronts.

DRUMACOO (D8; O.S.14, M 40 17) Small early church built into C13 church.

HIGH ISLAND (A7; O.S.10, L 50 57) Church, cells, slabs in cashel. Arrange boat journey at Cleggan.

INCHAGOIL (C7; O.S.11, M 13 49) Two churches (Romanesque work) and slabs. Island in Lough Corrib: arrange boat journey at Oughterard.

KILMACDUAGH (D9; O.S.14, M 40 00)   Fine round tower and several churches of different dates.

KILTIERNAN (D8; O.S.14, M 44 16)   Large stone enclosure with radial subdivisions surrounds early church.

ST MACDARA'S ISLAND (B8; O.S.10, L 72 30)   Church with unusual feature of *antae* continuing to roof ridge; cross-slabs. Boat journey from Carna.

TUAM (D7; O.S.11, M 44 52)   'Market Cross' in town centre made of pieces of C12 crosses. Fine Romanesque work incorporated in C19 cathedral.

CO. KERRY

AGHADOE (C12; O.S.21, V 93 93)   Round tower stump, C12 church and ogam stone.

ARDFERT (B11; O.S.21, Q 78 21)   Much Romanesque work.

CHURCH ISLAND, off Valencia Island (A13; O.S.20, V 43 79)   Excavated church, cells, cemetery, within small cashel. Boat from Caherciveen.

DUNLOE (C12; O.S.21, V 88 91)   Not a church site but worth visiting for ogam stones (not *in situ*).

GALLARUS (A12; O.S.20, Q 39 05)   Corbelled church, the only intact example.

ILLAUNTANNIG, Maharee Islands (B11; O.S.20, Q 62 21)   Churches, cells, graves in stone enclosure. Boat from Fahamore.

KILDREELIG (A13; O.S.20 inset, V 40 63)   Thick cashel with church, cells, souterrain and slabs, just below former school-house on Bolus Head.

KILLABUONIA (A13; O.S.20, V 40 70)   Hillside terraces with church, cells, graves and well.

KILMALKEDAR (A12; O.S.20, Q 40 06)   Romanesque church, alphabet stone, sundial, cross, ogam stone.

KILSHANNIG on Rough Point (B11; O.S.20, Q 63 20)   Graveyard with *chi-rho* slab.

RATTOO (C11; O.S.17, Q 88 33)   Round tower beside neglected church and graveyard.

REASK (A12; O.S.20, Q 37 04)   Cross-carved pillar and recently uncovered features including enclosure, church, cells and graves.

SKELLIG MICHAEL (A13; O.S.20 inset, V 25 61)   Unique group of churches, cells, graveyard, garden, on rocky peak. By boat in calm weather from Valencia, Portmagee, Derrynane, etc.

TEMPLE CASHEL (A13; O.S.20, V 37 69)   Partly ruined corbelled church; access across fields.

TEMPLE GEAL (A12; O.S.20, Q 40 03)   Ruined corbelled church, finial, ogam stone and graves.

CO. KILDARE

CASTLEDERMOT (J9; O.S.16, S 78 85)   C12 church door re-erected, round tower (top rebuilt), two granite crosses and several cross-carved stones.

KILLEEN CORMAC (J9; O.S.16, S 83 98)   Graveyard on mound with figure-carved pillar, ogam and cross-carved stones, in Colbinstown near Wicklow border.

MOONE (J9; O.S.16, S 79 93)   Very tall granite cross with figure carving; another base and part of cross nearby.

OLD KILCULLEN (J9; O.S.16, N 83 07)   Parts of three crosses; remains of C12 church and round tower.

CO. KILKENNY

CLONAMERY (H11; O.S.19, S 66 35)   W. end of church has *antae* and cross above door; added C12 chancel.

FRESHFORD (G10; O.S.18, S 41 65)   C12 W. front incorporated into C18 church. About 2 miles N., behind CLONTUBRID R.C. chapel, early gable finial built into wellhouse.

KILKIERAN (G11; O.S.18, S 42 27), KILLAMERY (G11; O.S.18, S 38 36) and KILREE (H11; O.S.18, S 49 41)   all have fine C8 or C9 crosses: Kilree also round tower and altered church.

CO. LAOIS

KILLESHIN (H10; O.S.19, S 67 78)   C12 church with fine W. door.

TIMAHOE (H9; O.S.16, S 53 90)   Round tower has elaborate Romanesque door.

CO. LIMERICK

ARDPATRICK (E11; O.S.22, R 64 21)   Slight remains of church and round tower in graveyard; superb hilltop site.

MUNGRET (E10; O.S.17, R 54 54)   Two churches remain from once-important settlement.

CO. LONDONDERRY see CO. DERRY

CO. LONGFORD

INCHCLERAUN (F7; O.S.12, M 99 59) Enclosure with several churches and slabs on island in Lough Ree: boats from Coosan Point or Elfleet Bay, Lanesborough, or from Athlone.

CO. LOUTH

MONASTERBOICE (J6; O.S.13, O 04 82)   Muiredach's Cross and the West Cross are two of the finest of all the crosses. One other cross, grave-slab and sundial. Round tower can be climbed; two churches, both later. Visit nearby Cistercian MELLIFONT (founded 1142) for the contrast.

CO. MAYO

CONG (C7; O.S.11, M 14 55)   C12 work in Augustinian abbey on or near early site.

DUVILLAUN MORE (B5; O.S.6, F 58 16), INISHGLORA (B5; O.S.6, F 62 31) and INISHKEA NORTH (B5; O.S.6, F 56 22)   Churches, cells, cross-slabs, enclosures, etc. All sea islands, reached by boat from Belmullet or Blacksod.

KILCUMMIN (D5; O.S.6, G 21 37)   Church, St Cummin's Grave and slabs, in Ballinlena.

KILLALA (D5; O.S.6, G 20 30)   Round tower and souterrain beside C. of I. cathedral.

MEELICK (D6; O.S.11, M 33 97) and TURLOUGH (D6; O.S.6, M 21 94)   have well-preserved round towers.

CO. MEATH

CASTLEKEERAN (H6; O.S.13, N 69 77)   Three fine plain crosses and base of fourth, ogam stone and cross-slab. Access beside farm and across field.

DONAGHMORE (J7; O.S.13, N 88 70)   Round tower (top restored) with Crucifixion carving above door; grave-slabs.

KELLS (H6; O.S.13, N 74 76)   At parish church are round tower, three crosses and slabs; to N.W. is Columcille's 'House', small stone-roofed church; to E. is Market Cross. A site not to be missed.

CO. MONAGHAN

CLONES (H5; O.S.8, H 50 26)   Ruined church, round tower and monumental tomb in graveyards, and cross in Diamond (made up of two).

CO. OFFALY

CLONMACNOIS (F8; O.S.15, N 01 31)   Wealth of churches, towers, crosses and slabs. Go E. along causeway to Nuns' Church and note glacial ridges (eskers) providing dry routes in generally low-lying area.

DURROW (G8; O.S.15, N 32 31)   Fine cross in dank grave-yard, also slabs. Access down drive to W. from T9 road.

GALLEN (F8; O.S.15, N 12 24)   Many slabs built into remains of medieval church on early site. Now in nunnery grounds: approach by private drive.

LEMANAGHAN (G8; O.S.15, N 17 27)   Ruined C12 church in graveyard. Causeway leads S.E. past well to overgrown enclosure with small early church. In BOHER R.C. church to N.E. at GROGAN is St Manchán's fine C12 metal shrine.

RAHAN (G8; O.S.15, N 26 25)   Two C12 churches (with C15 alterations) in large enclosure.

SEIRKIERAN (G9; O.S.15, N 14 02)   Impressive earthworks surround graveyard with cross-base, overgrown round tower and church ruin, S. of Clareen.

CO. SLIGO

DRUMCLIFF (E4; O.S.7, G 68 42)   Round tower stump and cross.

INISHMURRAY (E4; O.S.7, G 57 54)   One of best-preserved (though restored) monasteries with enclosure, churches, cells, slabs, etc. Sea island: boat journey to be arranged at Mullaghmore or Moneygold.

CO. TIPPERARY

AHENNY (G11; O.S.18, S 41 29)   Two fine C8 crosses and empty base.

CASHEL (F11; O.S.18, S 07 41)   Cormac's Chapel and cross, both C12, on rock with round tower and later buildings.

LIATHMORE (G10; O.S.18, S 22 58)   Two churches, recently uncovered round tower base, and extensive earthworks (not all Early Christian). Approached across fields.

MONAINCHA (G9; O.S.15, S 17 88)   Former island with C12 church and cross. Approached from minor road S. of T5, E. of Roscrea.

ROSCREA (G9; O.S.15, S 14 89)   C12 façade of cathedral, cross and round tower on main road from Dublin to Limerick.

ST BERRIHERT'S KYLE (F11; O.S.18, R 95 29)   Tiny (modern) enclosure in marshy field with rich collection of carved stones, in Ardane.

TOUREEN PEAKAUN (F11; O.S.18, S 01 28)   C12 church,

grave, crosses and many slabs. Not far from last site, close to railway line S. of T13, N.W. of Cahir.

CO. TYRONE

ARBOE (J3; O.S.4, H 96 76)   Fine tall cross W. of churchyard.

CLOGHER (H4; O.S.8, H 54 52)   Sundial in cathedral vestibule and two crosses to W. in graveyard.

DONAGHMORE (J4; O.S.4, H 77 65)   Figure-carved cross, made of parts of two crosses.

ERRIGAL KEEROGUE (H4; O.S.8, H 58 57)   Unfinished cross at ridge-top site.

CO. WATERFORD

ARDMORE (G13; O.S.22, X 19 77)   Fine late round tower, two churches and ogam stones.

CO. WESTMEATH

BEALIN (Twyford) (F8; O.S.12, N 10 43)   Cross with geometric, animal and figure carving, on hilltop.

FORE (H7; O.S.13, N 51 70)   Church with *antae* and carved cross over W. door; chancel added in about 1200. Remains of medieval abbey and town nearby.

INCHBOFIN (F7; O.S.12, N 06 55)   Two churches and good grave-slabs on island in Lough Ree. Boat from Coosan Point or Elfleet Bay, Lanesborough, or Athlone.

CO. WICKLOW

AGHOWLE (J10; O.S.19, S 93 69)   C12 church with fine W. door; plain cross.

GLENDALOUGH (K9; O.S.16, T 12 97)   Extensive, rich and beautiful site. Many churches, crosses, slabs, bullauns, etc. along valley from Upper Lake in W. to St Saviour's Priory in E. Conveniently reached from Dublin but often very crowded.

If you are staying in DUBLIN obvious places to visit, all within drives of one day, are MONASTERBOICE and KELLS, GLENDALOUGH, OLD KILCULLEN, MOONE and CASTLEDERMOT, and (a long day's drive) DURROW and CLONMACNOIS. In Dublin the NATIONAL MUSEUM and TRINITY COLLEGE LIBRARY should not be missed.

Index

Grid references are to the map between pages 2 and 3.

133

135